working in the mill
no more

working in the mill
no more

Text
Jan Breman

Photographs and Design
Parthiv Shah

AMSTERDAM UNIVERSITY PRESS

ISBN 90 5356 642 2

NUR 7560

Originally published in India in 2004 by Oxford University Press India, New Delhi.
First published in The Netherlands by Amsterdam University Press, Amsterdam.

© Oxford University Press India, 2004

This edition is distributed worldwide, excluding South Asia.

Acknowledgments

Many people helped and encouraged us to produce this photobook. First and foremost, we would like to express our gratitude to all those who we met, not once but repeatedly, and who consented to be photographed. It is our intention to find ways and means to show them the results of our encounters. If only for that purpose we aim to bring out a Gujarati edition of the book.

A wide range of contacts throughout the city enabled us to find more entry points than we already had, and to contextualise the accumulated data and images. To begin with, many grassroots activists engaged in various kinds of social work, among them Hausla Prasad Mishra, Rameshchandra Parmar, Valjibhai Patel, and Pirbhai Mansuri, kindly agreed to be our ears and eyes in the mill localities. They introduced us to ex-mill workers and other members of their households, spent time with us visiting neighbourhoods and guided us to sites where the victims of mass retrenchment assemble in search of new employment. In addition we got valuable information and advice from the staff of NGOs and educational institutions, as well as from members of the media. These brokers of civic action networks were always willing to facilitate our work and to point out what we should not miss. This category includes a number of old friends, including Manan Trivedi, Martin Macwan, Vidyut Joshi, Indukumar Jani, Achut Yagnik, Barry Underwood and Siddarth Darshan Kumar. We would also like to put on record our appreciation for the support provided by various agencies: in the first place, the veteran leaders and staff still present at the TLA office. This particularly applies to the Secretary-General, Manwar Shukla, who never tired of answering our queries and was happy to talk to us on many occasions about how the conditions of industrial labour were much better in the past. We feel no less indebted to Ela Bhatt and her associates in SEWA. While Elabehn energetically helped us to find out more about some of the historical photographs we had salvaged, Renana Jhabvala gave us some photos showing SEWA women engaged in collective action. Here again we feel most obliged to members of the local level cadre, especially Ramilabehn and Kapilabehn, who accompanied us on our frequent trips to their terrain of operation. We warmly thank B.B. Patel, who gave us access to the long lists of job dismissals in the archives of the Gandhi Labour Institute. He also arranged for us to attend a few training courses to meet ex-mill workers who were being given the chance to learn the basics of a new craft. Like all other rehabilitation schemes, this one has not been very successful, although the GLI staff did everything they could with the meagre resources placed at their disposal.

We would also like to express our gratitude to Natasha Awasthi, Mahendra Rathore and Niraj Pathak who assisted Parthiv Shah in the tedious process of designing a book out of a mass of unstructured data and prints, to Andy Brown who edited Jan Breman's text and captions, to Teun Bijvoet at the Amsterdam School of Social Science

Research (ASSR) for his handling of the project correspondence and administration and, last but not least, to Jose Komen who, as executive director of the ASSR, monitored the financial accounts and sent out early warnings when she found that we had exhausted our funds.

Finally, we would like to put on record the names of our sponsors who, at different stages of the project, were willing to contribute to the budget. At the outset the Regional Office of the International Labour Office in New Delhi provided a stipend that allowed us to start the preparatory work. The Centre for Media and Alternative Communication in Delhi gave us the valuable office space where we could spend hours working on the book.

HIVOS, a Dutch NGO with a branch office in Bangalore, supported us with a generous grant to cover the cost of production. The budget for this was much higher than had been foreseen since, because of other work assignments, we had to split the project up into a total of six rounds in the course of 2001. These breaks in our schedule actually had unanticipated advantages because each time we were forced to take stock of the outcome of the previous round and to carefully plan what to do in the next one. But it also complicated our agenda, because we had to travel, either separately or jointly, to Ahmedabad more times than initially planned. We could not have foreseen, of course, that the outbreak of communal riots at the end of February 2002 would compel us to return to the city on four more occasions to cover the tragedy and its impact, the final trip being completed only in early December last year. HIVOS, ILO and a fund for small grants administered by the University of Amsterdam took care of the expenses incurred by this unexpected extension of the project for ten difficult months, for which of course no provision had been made in the original budget.

Two other agencies, the Dutch trade union federation FNV and the Indo-Dutch Programme on Alternatives in Development (IDPAD), provided a subsidy which enabled us to make this book available at the lowest possible price, to ensure that it will be used for training courses given in India by NGOs and trade unions, and for teaching in schools of social work. Part of this grant is meant to be spent on photo exhibitions at the time of the book's launch.

Once the project is formally completed, the total stock of photos, published and unpublished, together with the data required for their identification, will be deposited in the collection of oral history at the V.V. Giri National Labour Institute in Noida, India.

Jan Breman
Parthiv Shah
Amsterdam/ New Delhi, August 2003

Contents

Map of Industrial Ahmedabad in early 20th Century

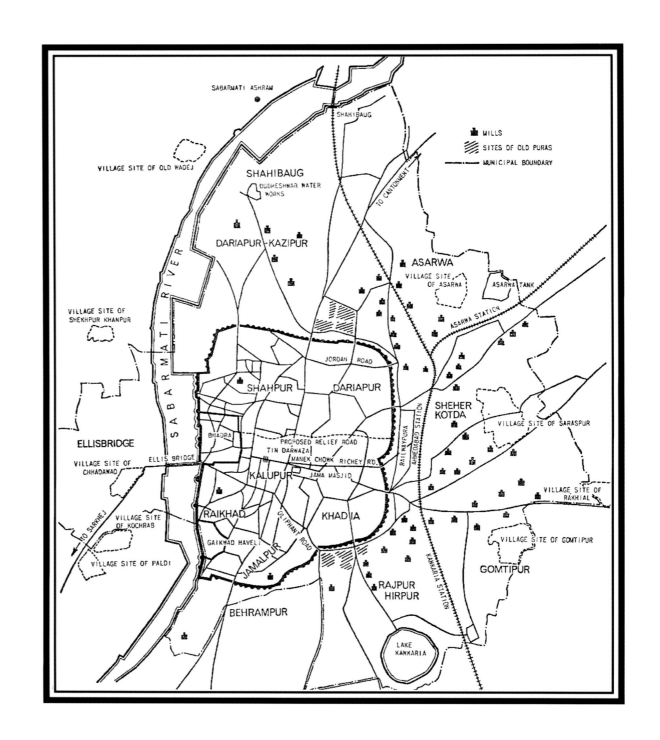

Introduction

Jan Breman

When I started my research on labour in Gujarat more than forty years ago the study of urban and industrial employment was not an attractive option. The large majority of the people at the bottom of the economy had always worked in agriculture and were very much village based. A monograph on agricultural labour was the outcome of my first fieldwork in 1961-2. Outmigration became a recurrent theme of my investigations in the years that followed and I stayed close to the landless workers who left their native place for a couple of weeks, many months or several years in search of income away from home. Their mobility was usually circular in nature and sometimes, but certainly not always, urban directed. Even the minority among them which managed to settle down permanently in towns or cities together with other members of the same household, rarely succeeded to work their way up in the labour hierarchy. In the urban habitat these newly arrived were absorbed as self-employed or casual wage earners in the informal sector of the economy. Few held illusions about ever being able to find steady jobs with protected and decent conditions of employment including social provisions. Most of them also did not participate in the kind of collective action with which a small industrial vanguard of higher skilled and better paid workers demonstrated their assertion for a life of security and dignity. The trade union movement, which already came up early in the twentieth century, has only in exceptional cases expanded its reach beyond the formal sector of the economy.

Would the offspring of informal sector workers be better off? This was, of course, the pledge held out by politicians and policy makers in their post-Independence design for a bright future, more concretely laid down in elaborate drafts on how to shape an industrial type of society out of an agrarian one. The gains made so far by a small and privileged segment of the total workforce were in the near future going to be shared and result in a better life for all. Is this indeed what has happened or is happening? I have put my doubts and worries on record in a series of publications around the turn of the century which deal with the footloose proletariat kept in a transient state between countryside and city as well as between various economic sectors.[1] Another outcome of my research was a photobook published on the assumption that public opinion would or should care about the plight of men and women, adults and children stuck at the lower end of the urban and rural economy. Co-authored with Arvind N. Das and Ravi Agarwal, Down and Out; Labouring under Global Capitalism (Oxford University Press, New Delhi 2000) makes an attempt to visualise the new and cruel labour regime that has emerged in the flawed transition from a peasant to an industrial way of life.

The present book can be seen as a follow-up to this earlier document, mixing narrative and image, and is produced to inform a wide audience on what happens when labour standards drop all of a sudden to a much lower level and labour rights are forfeited. In 1998 I started to do research on the collapse of the well-established and large-scale textile industry in Ahmedabad. Since the late 1970s the mills had closed down, one after the other, resulting in loss of jobs for a huge workforce. How did the victims experience what must have been a major crisis in their life, based until then on regular, secure and relatively well-paid employment? Which were the coping mechanisms that helped them to overcome, or not, this dramatic setback? On dismissal the large majority of the mill workforce instantly slid down to the informal sector of the economy. Apart from a sharp fall in income, the shift in material well-being could not but have an adverse effect on their social consciousness. The mental change became manifest in loss of dignity and representation. The economic and political space needed for collective action, which for decades had been spearheaded by a powerful trade union to which most of them belonged, disappeared overnight. The fall from workers' paradise - which meant holding a secure, skilled and protected job in the formal sector - has had far-reaching repercussions at the household and neighbourhood level. I gave a lot of attention to these features in my successive rounds of fieldwork which lasted until the end of 2000. The outcome of this research is elaborated upon in a separate monograph, to be published simultaneously with this book: The making and unmaking of an industrial working class (Oxford University Press and Amsterdam University Press, New Delhi/Amsterdam 2003).

While going around in the city, and in the mill localities in particular, I endeavoured to meet a lot people well-informed about the theme of my interest. This was how I came to know about Parthiv Shah who had already started making photos when mill workers were dismissed in large numbers during the early 1980s. When I happened to get hold of a collage put together by him, kept with other documents in a collection at the Gandhi Labour Institute, the idea came to me to follow up on his set of portraits:

of workers still operating the looms and other machines in the mills, about the street protests when they lost their jobs, their anger on realising that industrialists, government bureaucrats and union bosses were unwilling and unable to turn the tide or at least to protect their rights, the futile search for regular jobs and the despair about the politics of exclusion to which they with other members of their households were now exposed. After I had tracked Parthiv down and we discovered that we already knew about each other, we immediately agreed to produce a photobook depicting conditions of work and life before and after the massive eviction from mill employment which was still going on when we started our joint venture.

Once I had completed my own research – based in 1998 on a survey and continued in 1999-2000 in the form of anthropological fieldwork in selected neighbourhoods – Parthiv and I returned to the same mill localities and often to the same informants I had met before. Above all to seek their permission and help for making photos in which either they themselves or relatives and neighbours figure prominently. We started shooting in the beginning of 2001 with Kiran Nanavati as a constant member of our team. My associate in the prior research, Kiran was well acquainted with the local scene which we had come to know during the preceding two years. He took charge of our day-to-day schedule and planned in advance where to go and whom to meet. Most important of all, Kiran closely monitored the photos made, by writing down particulars of all the persons interviewed. His files have enabled us to identify the people and the places you are looking at in the book. It goes without saying that only a small sample of the pictures taken can be reproduced here, perhaps one out of every twenty prints made. One criterion more important than any other in our final selection has been our duty to present a balanced view, to bring in all features essential for highlighting the plight of ex-mill workers and the need to back up our story with telling illustrations. We interrupted our explorations in the mill areas with attempts to go in search of photos made at the time when Ahmedabad earned the proud reputation of having grown into the Manchester of India. The high point of our quest came when we climbed down to the dust-covered cellar in the trade union building where piles of photos had been dumped in dirty gunny sacks and were now turning to waste. Coughing and cursing Parthiv chose whatever he thought would be useful for our purpose. The union peon who had been sent along to find out and report back what had been forgotten helped us by randomly tearing out of albums photos on which he thought to recognise the venerable heroes of past struggle and glory. We also paid visits to commercial shops from which veteran photographers, next to their bread-and-butter business of filming marriage parties, kept track of major events in the city for their own pleasure. These expeditions sourcing for the visual history of Ahmedabad have enabled us to document work in and life around the mills in better times. An era which is only kept alive in the wistful memories of the victims of large-scale de-industrialisation.

In early 2002, our mission seemed to have been completed successfully. By the middle of January, we had captured the last remaining images and, in the first week of February, after having dealt with a few loose ends which needed documentation, I was all set to leave Ahmedabad. Only to return a little over a month later, when the communal riots which brought Gujarat to the attention of the world at large raged on unabated. The word riots actually suggests a kind of evenhandedness which was completely lacking. With the complicity of the state government a pogrom unfolded, carried out by activists mobilised by the leading political party and with the Muslim minority as its target. The powers that be justified the carnage as a spontaneous reaction to a criminal act in which 58 persons, most of them Hindu pilgrims, were burnt alive in a train near Godhra station. In the backlash initiated by the Hindutva forces, which lasted for several weeks, many more people were killed often in indescribable ways. The authorities did not even bother to put their excact number on record. It was clear that we could not remain silent on these gruesome events and their aftermath in a book narrating and illustrating the changes in the composition of the city's economy and its workforce over the last few decades. In a short essay which appeared in a prominent weekly, I pointed out that there was indeed a relationship between the recurrent explosions of religious violence in Ahmedabad since the early 1980s and major ruptures in the social fabric of the city. In my understanding the downward mobility of the army of ex-mill workers did not merely result in their impoverishment or even pauperisation, but also created new social and political fault lines. Vested interests are engaged in reshaping communal identities and in fanning the flames of confrontation between the newly aligned coalition of loyalties. We decided to return to the locale of our fieldwork and without loosing sight of our main focus – the miserable fate of ex-mill workers – to find out what had happened to our informants during the riots. Our interaction with members of the religious majority and minority revolved around the memories of their shared past as formal sector labourers, as the rank and file of the same trade union, united also in casting their vote for the same political party and living together in the same neighbourhoods. This fabric of commonalty has been brutally torn apart. We found back those on the receiving end in relief camps, to which tens of thousands had escaped from an ordeal which an estimated two thousand – irrespective of gender and age – did not survive. The people we spoke to had lost homes or other property, and still did not know whether they would eventually be allowed to go back to the places where they had lived before the explosion of hate. Victimised once again these people face a future even darker than when they lost their mill jobs. In our view, and that is the essence of the story we tell, informalisation of employment and social marginalisation, compounded by the politics of communal segregation, are parallel sides of the same dynamics. That is, progressive exclusion from mainstream society.

[1] Wage hunters and gatherers; search for work in the urban and rural economy of south Gujarat. Oxford University Press, New Delhi 1994; Footloose labour; working in India's informal economy. Cambridge University Press, Cambridge 1996; the first and last chapter in: The worlds of Indian industrial labour (edited with J.P. Parry and K. Kapadia). Sage Publications, New Delhi 1999; The labouring poor in India; patterns of exploitation, subordination and exclusion. Oxford University Press, New Delhi 2002.

Unprecedented unemployment haunts city

Continued from Page 1 Column 3

the Jagat Mill was closed down a year ago. Her husband was getting Rs. 16 a day in the mill. Bhanuben and her children now make garments but the day-long toil brings in only Rs. 3 a day. The total earning last month was only Rs. 92.

vill — shmlords. Most of the slum dwellers are in the clutches of a ruthless jshmlords who would not hesitate to throw out the families if the latter did not pay.

If this is the lot of textile mill workers, the condition of the workers in the unorganised ... worse.

ed by the closed mills have become casual labourers, kerosene, fruits and vegetable vendors, cart-pullers and rickshaw-drivers.

To add insult to injury, the zealous corporation and police authorities have uprooted several hundred poor lari-gallawallas in the wake of the jaundice scare. They gave vent to ...

bread. "A thousand people of our own union have lost their livelihood", Mr. Ashok Punjabi, president of the lari-galla ladat amidji, claimed.

Maseribhai, a displaced textile worker on Nareda Road has a bag lari. The anti-jaundice squad came along and removed it with all its valuables.

Revumal Udavdas (50) had been ...

બે માસુમ બાળકો સાથે
બેકાર કામદારની પત્નીની આત્મહત્યા

બે દિવસથી બાળકો, ભૂખે ટળવળતાં હતાં:
બાપુનગર વિસ્તારની કરુણ ઘટના

---

2 more city mills closed down

By A Staff Reporter

AHMEDABAD, June 18.

THE crisis in the textile industry, today further deepened with the closure of two more mills in the city. One mill has already closed down three days ago, bringing the total to 17 so far.

workers than they need not report for duty and that they would be paid their wages. The notices, put up before the start of the first shift, said that the mills were facing financial ... colties and it was not possible to run them. However, the workers would be entitled to their wages ...

ment is empowered to launch criminal prosecution against the agents of industrial units closing their establishment without giving three months' notice to the government. The textile mills and industrial units, covered by the industrial disputes Act, also cannot lay off or retrench workers ...

Prayer to Kali on behalf of workers

By A Staff Reporter

AHMEDABAD, June 18: Workers belonging to the Bharatiya Kamdar parishad today adopted a novel method of seeking relief for those workers rendered jobless due to closure of textile mills in the state.

Nearly 2,000 workers affiliated to the memorandum Party, submitted a memorandum to Godden Kali at Bhadra here, seeking her blessings for the reopening of the mills. The workers prayed the goddess to bless them so that they ...

આજે મિલ કામદારો રક્ત લિખિત આવેદનપત્ર આપશે

કાગળ પર મિલો સરકાર બેવકુફ બના...

આજે મિલ કામદારો

સારંગપુર મિલના બંધ આમરણાંત મજૂરના ઉપવાસનો ૧૨મો દિવસ

અમદાવાદ, શનિવાર.

૨૧મીએ મેઘાણી નગરથી અસારવા વિસ્તાર બંધનુ એલાન

અમદાવાદ, મંગળવાર.

પેટલાદની ગૃજેશ મીલ ૬૦૦ માણસો બે...

બધ મિલોના પ્રશ્ને આજે અશ્વમેધ યજ્ઞ

અમદાવાદ, સોમવાર.

One more city mill closes

By A Staff Reporter

AHMEDABAD, May 19. One more city mill, the Commercial Ahmedabad Mills Co. Ltd. was closed today rendering 2,500 workers jobless, the company did not pay their electricity bill.

A press release issued by the Textile Labour Association said that it was filed... against the illegal closure of the mill for the workers' are not paid wages. With the closure of this mill the number of closed mills in the city has gone up to 13.

The TLA has drawn the attention of the Union commerce minister, Mr. V. P. Singh, and the state government to the closure of thousands of workers ...

getting any assistance for self-employment from agencies like district industrial centre and the state tries despite ...job security assurance.

The state government had decided to open a joint cell of Labour Industry and finance department cials to provide assistance to the employed mill workers. Even this is not yet been set up. ... sion to provide 150 auteri... the mills workers had been ... in the city for the last four months.

Two hurt in attack on Majoor Mahajan office

By A Staff Reporter

AHMEDABAD, June 19.

AGITATED workers of two closed mills today ransacked the office of the Textile Labour Association (Majoor Mahajan) here, a posse of policemen rushed to the spot and brought the situation under control.

Two people were injured in what they have described as a first instance of violence over mill closure and the association, known for settling disputes through Gandhian way.

According to an association source, the trouble started when representatives of two mills — the Manchester Mill and New Swadeshi — assembled at the hall of the Majoor Mahajan yesterday to discuss the matters time out of the closure of the two mills.

They shout slogans and broke away broke some furniture and files in the office ...

મજૂર મહાજન સંઘની કચેરીમાં ટોળા દ્વારા ભાંગફોડ

ઉપવાસી મિલ કામદારની તબિયત બગડતાં હોસ્પિટલમાં

બધ મિલોના પ્રશ્ને

Introduction

Parthiv Shah

It was 1982. I was a student in Ahmedabad at the National Institute of Design, specializing in Visual Communication. During one of the communication exercises, we had to deal with an issue that required more use of photographs than text. After shooting, we had to do a layout in a similar fashion as the photo features that the erstwhile Illustrated Weekly used to run in every issue. I selected "textile mills" as my subject for the exercise. Now, after many years, I am wondering why I chose the subject of textile mills and mill workers. Maybe because Ahmedabad was known as the Manchester of India. Besides, Ahmedabad is the city where I grew up. Or just maybe because I thought that this is the kind of subject that will lend itself to interesting photography and that these pictures could be used by magazines or newspapers as they would reflect a real "issue". I probably felt the pictures would one day transcend the boundaries of a typical, cast-iron communication exercise that I was undertaking.

It was difficult to decide where to start from — the mill or the mill-worker. I went to an area known as the 'Captain' area, which is behind the Ahmedabad railway station. There I met a Muslim mill-worker, Azizbhai, who was the workers' representative in one of the mills, which was under a lock out. It was almost evening so I came back. But from the next day onwards, I started visiting that place. It will be a fitness of things to mention here that even after I finished my communication exercise, I kept returning to that place at regular intervals as I got personally involved with the lives and times of the workers — their movement to fight against the lock outs in mills. I

photographed the mills, the protest rallies and the homes of the workers for almost 2 years. I tried to document the moments of trials and tribulations; the changes occurring in their daily lives through different seasons and festivals; situations that were impacting their lives, culture and environment.

Some of these pictures were published by a couple of magazines but most of them remained in my archives. However, In 2001, I met Professor Jan Breman in Delhi. During this meeting, he expressed a desire to see the photographs of the textile mill workers I took in the 1980s. (I already knew about Professor Breman and his work, especially on South Gujarat for my father's family comes from that region of the state). Professor Breman and I discussed how we should approach the subject after 20 years as well as the subject of his study. For the next two years, I visited Ahmedabad frequently photographing the mill area, the workers and their *Chali*. I also photographed workers with new jobs and workers who were very sick with different kinds of ailments. A partially-functioning textile mill – where a power-loom unit and a processing unit were flouting all labour and environmental laws — was also captured on film by me only after I could convince the mill owners that nowhere in print would their names appear.

Photography can be an act of non-intervention but sometimes intervention is inevitable. Memorable scoops of contemporary photo-journalism like the picture of a Vietnamese reaching for a gasoline can, or an unemployed mill worker in Ahmedabad dying of bysinosis, is born out of a situation where a photographer is experiencing an event and not just recording an image.

I took many photographs in keeping with the text which Professor Breman had in mind. But it is always difficult for a practitioner of the visual medium, such as myself, to have pictures that strictly adhere to the text. In this case, however, we were not embarking upon bringing out a mere photo book but a book which could be appreciated by both academicians and experts on the subject as well as those who love photographs. I have always believed that photographs are experiences, not just images which remain static. A photograph is timeless yet the time and the context decide how one experiences it. What is visible always gives time to cross the boundaries of the first sub-conscious experience. Photography captures a thin slice of space and time — a fraction of a second. In this project, my attempt was to record the change which is occurring very fast in the industrial area of Ahmedabad. The nature of change is anthropogenic in this case and therefore it is difficult for the people and their environment to adapt to it. A medium such as photography can tell the tale as it is meant to record images and events in a single frame or in a continuous mode. Photography itself has a problem of rendering a three dimensional environment into two. As a result of this, capturing the spirit of a situation through the lens becomes an arduous task. A photographer is not just a recorder who codes and decodes but an interpreter as well. I sincerely hope that these images than can be interpreted by various experts to decode messages relevant to them and their own realm of work.

Our perception of 'The Situation' is now more and more being articulated by the camera's intervention. An event will end but the picture will still exist, conferring on the event a kind of immortality and importance it would otherwise never have enjoyed. While real people are out there getting removed from their jobs, the photographer stays behind his camera, creating a tiny element of another world: the image world that bids to outlast us all, and lives beyond traces of moments which can assist the present and the future generation study the problem from an another angle — a visual one. There have not been many visual studies undertaken in India. This project tries to take the viewer from the 1930's to 2003 with the help of some additional photographs which we found in poor condition in the offices of Textile Labour Association (TLA). A few others were obtained from the well-known photographer from Ahmedabad, Pranlal Patel.

I took up the subject keeping in mind that here are people who have their own way of living in the world and looking at it. As a photographer, who has also worked in the field of visual communication, I used my skills to communicate the untold tales of a city. It was relatively easy for me as I grew up in Ahmedabad. To the mill workers, I was not an outsider that a photographer usually is. For me, in a sense, it meant re-visiting my roots. The photographic moment for me was a historical one.

The Manchester of India

Pre-colonial Gujarat was renowned in South Asia and beyond as a centre for cotton growing and processing. A wide variety of other textiles were also produced, including silk, velvet, satin, and brocade. These fabrics were sold on the domestic market and shipped to other countries in Asia and Europe. Spinning and weaving took the form of home-based industry in town and countryside. The production of high-quality textiles like brocade, in which gold and silver thread were used, was concentrated in *karkhanas,* workshops in which artisans were employed under the direct supervision of owners-entrepreneurs.

In 1861, Ranchodlal Chhotalal, from a prominent family of Nagar Brahmins in Ahmedabad, opened the first steam-driven cotton mill in the city. The number of employees of the Ahmedabad Spinning and Weaving Company grew from an original 63 to 300 in 1864 and 500 in 1867. After a relatively slow start, the number of mills financed with local capital grew rapidly The *swadeshi* movement, launched in 1905 as an early expression of economic nationalism which urged people to buy locally produced goods, considerably strengthened the budding textile industry and the class of domestic entrepreneurs it spawned. The Ahmedabad Millowners Association was originally set up in 1891 to represent their interests against the colonial authorities. But, from an early stage, the owners also used this collective platform to oppose demands from the rapidly growing industrial proletariat for an improvement in working conditions. From the early 20th century onwards Ahmedabad came to be known as the Manchester of India.

The Birth of an Industrial Workforce

 ▲ ▶

Although textile production in Ahmedabad became mill-based, artisanal manufacture – for example of temple cloth and women's wear – continued throughout the 20th century. As a traditional craft, production of these fabrics survived in small workshops within the walls of the old city.

At work in the mill

The first generation of mill workers was recruited from a broad range of city dwellers mainly belonging to the lower castes. There was no lack of interest in working in the new industry but, as the capacity of the mills gradually expanded, the supply of labour available in the *bazar* economy of Ahmedabad was eventually exhausted. The owners were forced to search for a new source of labour outside the urban economy. They found this in the surrounding countryside among Muslims and members of castes stigmatized as untouchables who until then had made a living as landpoor and landless peasants in the rural economy. Jobbers recruited menfolk, and often entire households, from these subaltern strata to work in the mills. While the new urban proletariat in other parts of the country seemed reluctant to sever their ties with the mode of work and life they had left behind in the villages, the industrial workforce in Ahmedabad adapted to its new urban habitat very quickly. By the end of the 1920s, four out of five workers in the modern textile sector had been born or brought up either in or in the close proximity of the city.

The work in the mills was determined by the caste identity which the workers had brought with them to the city. Dheds and Vankars, who used to supplement their income from farm labour by weaving, were put to work in the spinning shops, as were the Chamars, a leather-tanning caste. These *harijans* were unable to find work in the weaving shops. As latecomers to the mills, they found this more skilled and therefore better paid work was already the domain of Muslims and intermediate-caste Hindus like the Kanbis.

Labour was a commodity which the industrialists preferred to make use of with no restriction whatsoever. Leave was not a right but a favour that was arbitrarily granted, depending on the mood of the gang-boss. From the opening of the first mill, Sunday was kept free as a day of rest. But even this recess was restricted, as many of the workers had to go to the mill for a few hours to clean the machines and the workplace. Illness or family events were not considered a good enough reason to take time off. Absence in the case of births, marriages or death was not tolerated and was considered a failure to fulfil the duty to work. Workers committing such an offence would have their wages withheld, and would be lucky to get away without further sanctions being imposed. It would be untrue, however, to imply that the workforce acquiesced in this regime of relentless subjugation. It was quite usual for them to miss one or two days' work after receiving their two-weekly wage. The bonus offered by employers to discourage this practice had little or no effect. Sick pay was unheard of and medical costs were reimbursed only if they were incurred as a result of the work, for example in the not so rare cases of industrial accidents. As the workers got older, their health deteriorated and few were able to push on after the age of 40 or 45. Many were so worn out that they chose, or were forced, to give up their jobs even earlier.

Because the piece-rated wages from the mill were not enough to maintain a wife and children, they too had to become involved in the industrial process. Muslim women were spared the factory regime, because of the taboo on their working outside the home. There were also very few women from the

higher Hindu castes, whose presence on the shopfloor was seen as a violation of the strict rules of virtuous conduct expected of them. But low-caste women worked in the mills, taking with them small children who had to be breastfed. The infants were kept quiet for the whole day with doses of afim (opium).

Child labour, too, was widespread in the modern textile industry in Ahmedabad. Unable to make ends meet on their own paltry income, parents used to wake up their youngsters at dawn, either by sprinkling water on their faces or by beating them if they refused to rise. Many parents were forced to extract a full day's work from their very young sons. Since the Factories Act (1891) only permitted boys to be employed for half a day, they were sent to work in two different mills to circumvent the restriction.

Production in the mills was split up into a number of different activities which, as already mentioned, were often divided among the workers along caste and religious lines. Workers were trained by their already skilled mates for jobs which changed little, if at all, over the years. Practically the only promotion mill hands could achieve was the conversion of their temporary contract as badli workers into permanent ones. In very exceptional cases, they might make it to the position of a jobber, but that was as far as it went.

At the end of the day women came to collect the waste dumped in the mill ground to use for the manufacture of patchwork at home.

Production went on without regular breaks and without canteen or toilet facilities. The machines were kept running and only by stepping in for each other could the workers take a rest, eat the food brought from home and go out for a smoke or a cup of tea. Absence from constant duty was not tolerated and employers blamed workers for 'loitering'.

In marketing their products the Ahmedabad industrialists appealed to customers only to buy cloth made in India.

RUSTOM MILLS
AHMEDABAD

Living in squalor

Equally miserable as the conditions under which the first generation of mill workers had to work were the circumstances in which they were forced to live. They built their own shelters, initially made from mud with a straw roof, on open wasteland outside the old city and as close as possible to the mill, where they were corralled for at least twelve hours a day. They had to survive in these hutments for many years without even the most elementary facilities, such as paved roads, sewers, a water supply, refuse collection, or public lighting. The population of these sprawling settlements, known as *wadas*, was divided according to caste and religion; the segregation within the mill walls was thus duplicated outside. In 1911, Ahmedabad had a population of nearly 214,000, a rise of more than 80 per cent compared to 40 years ago. This increase was almost entirely due to the textile industry, which quickly began to leave a clear mark on the city's economy. The industrial districts, where work and everyday life overlapped, remained concentrated on the left bank of the Sabarmati river, forming a semi-circle around the old city. From the very start, these neighbourhoods looked like slums and accounted for a large majority of the 84,375 dwellings counted in Ahmedabad in 1911. The jerry-built housing in this part of the city (most of the dwellings were simple huts) was marked by a high degree of poverty, together with other problems that inevitably accompany such a state of deprivation.

Around the turn of the century, the mill owners, who initially accepted no responsibility at all for housing their workers, started to build *chalis*, or chawls (walk-throughs). These were alleyways lined with one or two-room dwellings, which the workers could rent at a low rate. In 1899, the city authorities also started providing factory workers with these kinds of tenements, as part of a building plan that closely resembled the 'coolie lines' constructed on plantations and in mining enclaves. These single storey barrack-like dwellings, grouped along narrow, deadend alleys around the mills, became increasingly popular in the 20th century and eventually dominated the industrial districts as they became more and more densely populated. The inhabitants of many chawls were subject to the control of the nearby mills, not only as workers but as tenants. This extension of the authority of the employers outside the confines of the factory gates intensified the dependence which the industrialists believed necessary to ensure discipline among the workers.

▶ ▲

A house in *Vaghri vas*, one of the neighbourhoods that came up in the mill area. The self-built tenements did not have proper access roads or basic amenities such as drainage, electricity, and tap water. In the early period the *kachha* style of housing together with the low population density suggested a habitat which was still more rural than urban.

The early struggle for emancipation

The factory workers at times attempted to escape from the rigid discipline imposed on them through short spurts of collective action. The unrest, known as *hullad*, always broke out unexpectedly and was usually restricted to an individual department or mill, but would sometimes unleash a wave of resistance that swept through all the industrial neighbourhoods and could even disrupt the economic life of the entire city. The large strikes were not always aimed at achieving pay rises or other improvements in working conditions, but also broke out in protest at measures announced by the employers and which were seen as making the situation worse. An example is the protest by women in 1891, when they were threatened with dismissal as a result of the new regulations restricting their working hours. In 1895, a major strike broke out when the employers switched from a system of weekly payment to twice a month. And in 1899, the mills were forced to close their gates again after the owners had taken advantage of an influx of new workers from Rajasthan and Saurasthra, where there was a famine, to announce wage cuts. The founding of the Ahmedabad Millowners Association in 1891 was both the cause and effect of the growing agitation at the end of the 19th century. However, the workers were often unable to close ranks to defend their common interests. They may have been united by a common bond but the industrial action this inspired was usually unsuccessful.

The champions of liberation from colonial domination understood that their struggle could succeed only if they mobilized the support of the mass of the people. This led in 1906 to the formation of the Swadeshi Mitra Mandal in the city. Its activities included holding evening classes for mill workers, and indicates the growing awareness among the bourgeoisie that the struggle for national independence would have to be accompanied by social reform. Anasuyaben Sarabhai, the sister of one of the leading industrial magnates in the city, was a prominent advocate of this school of thought. In 1914, Ambalal Sarabhai gave his sister permission to set up a school for the children of the mill workers, in a chawl which he owned and which was located close to one of his mills. Many years later she recounted her memories to an audience of workers:

Gandhi addressing the mill workers during the 1918 strike. Anasuyaben is sitting next to him. The bungalow in the background is the residence of Ambalal Sarabhai, the leading captain of industry in the city.

I opened a small school in Amarpura for teaching your children. Working among you I began to understand your dreadful condition. The picture of men and women making their way home after working for 24 to 36 hours in the mill is still vivid before my eyes. Even small children were compelled to work for 12 hours then!…We noticed before us emaciated and despondent children, their bodies naked and covered with dirt and unkempt hair. We commenced our work in right earnest.

The expansion of the textile industry gathered momentum with the outbreak of the First World War. Domestic sales increased as imports of clothing from Lancashire ceased, while production for other markets in Asia experienced spectacular growth. The extremely high profits made by the mill owners during these years may be seen as an indication of the low wages. The employers were forced, however, to grant a bonus in mid-1917, when workers threatened to leave the city en masse after an outbreak of the plague. To induce them to stay, mill owners offered them a premium of 70 per cent of their regular pay. When the epidemic was over the employers announced that they were going to abolish the plague bonus, but raise original wage levels somewhat. The offer they made was by no means enough to compensate for the increased cost of living during the war years. Anasuyaben declared herself willing to help the workers in the struggle for justice. Her brother, the city's leading captain of industry, was aware that further concessions would be inevitable if industrial conflict were to be avoided. As president of the employers' association he contacted Gandhi, who had settled in Ahmedabad in 1915 after his return from South Africa. The strike which broke out in February 1918 was the result of the refusal of the employers to increase wages by more than 20 per cent and their resolute rejection of the workers' claim for a 50 per cent pay raise. Gandhi agreed to arbitrate if both sides showed themselves willing to abide by the decision of a small committee. This panel included a few representatives of the employers, while he himself and two of his trusted associates would represent the interests of the workers. Since the mill owners refused to give in, Gandhi announced that he would fast unto the death as a final attempt to get his compromise accepted. The employers had little other choice than to agree to a 35 per cent increase in wages. The 'righteous struggle' had been won, for the time being.

Supported by a group of young volunteers and with the permission of her brother Anasuyaben started literacy classes in 1914 for adults and children in the mill localities.

The Gandhian model

Mahatma Gandhi's view of the relationship between capital and labour was based on his rejection of the industrial system in Western society. The settlement of disputes through a willingness to compromise, through negotiation rather than confrontation, and, by implication, the acceptance of arbitration and a commitment to abide by its outcome, were the core features of the trade union which Gandhi founded for the mill workers of Ahmedabad at the end of the First World War. Adhering to these principles, however, not only made dealing with the employers extremely difficult, but also demanded a great effort on the part of the union's leaders to instil into their members the discipline that they were said to lack. The union, named Majoor Mahajan Sangh, was founded on 25 February 1920, nearly 30 years after the employers had set up their association. The new union appointed Anasuyaben president for life.

Trade Unionism

Early issues of *Majoor Sandesh,* the TLA periodical.

◀

Anasuyaben with Shamprasad Vasavada (Gen. Secretary) and Noor Mohammed Sheikh (Secretary) of the TLA in the early 1950s.

▶

Khandushai Desai addressing mill workers. In the background the TLA office housed in the former residence of Ambalal Sarabhai.

Hygiene and health care instruction in the early 1950s.

A typical mill *chali*

The MMS, known in English as the Textile Labour Association (TLA), was from the very beginning an association of craft-based unions of spinners, weavers, thrustle workers, folders, sizers, winders, card, blow and frame room workers, drivers, oilmen, and firemen. Together, they all became members of the same federation. Gandhi imposed a code of good conduct on the working class and the union's programme of activities placed great emphasis on the education of the workers as obedient employees aware of their social responsibility in general and their duty towards the employers in particular. The 'righteous struggle', which had already booked its first success, was not just about better pay. The employers were also forced to accept a shorter working day, reduced from 12 to 10 hours, and were no longer permitted to employ children under the age of 12. Going on strike, however, was abandoned as a means of improving the lot of the workers.

The TLA avoided confrontation with the employers and gave priority to raising the quality of life in the residential areas. Gandhian activists were deeply impressed by the need to drastically improve the living conditions of average mill worker and their families. In the popular view, the dire poverty of the workers was the result of all kinds of bad habits, such as alcohol abuse, gambling, an obstinate tendency to spend more than they earned, a severe lack of hygiene in regard to themselves and their homes, and a general intemperance and lack of sobriety. These defects in their behaviour were seen to extend to relations between men and women and a neglect on the part of adults to give the next generation a solid and decent upbringing. To bring about a change in this state of immorality at the base of society was a civilizing mission, in which both those fighting for national freedom and reformers of religious persuasion found them- selves in Gandhi's campaign for social upliftment.

The TLA devoted 70 per cent of its budget in 1925 to social care and welfare schemes. Surprisingly, given the bad quality of housing, improving accommodation was not a priority. No effort was made to promote public housing through the foundation of working-class cooperatives. The workers remained dependent on the chawls built around the mills and rented out by the mill owners themselves or by private landlords. The limited size of the shelters provided and the lack of even the most basic facilities, such as drinking water and sewage, made housing one of the biggest obstacles to efforts to improve the workers' living standards. In 1924, the first mill worker was elected to the city council as a member of Congress. The union leadership took the initiative to nominate the man, a spinner from an untouchable caste, as candidate and carefully guided him in the election campaign. In 1937, a quarter of the members of the city council were members of the TLA. Only a few were workers, the majority being union officials. This growth in the political representation of labour helped to alert the urban bureaucracy to the needs and wishes of the residents of the mill localities, which had long been discriminated against in the allocation of municipal funds.

The union contributed to the welfare of its members by introducing urgently needed health care provisions. In 1921, child mortality was as high as 360 per 1,000 in the industrial districts, compared to 50 per 1,000 among the population of Ahmedabad as a whole. The physical conditions of the people working in the mills was also much worse than in the city at large. The opening of the first two primary health centres, for consultation and the free distribution of medicines for workers and their families, offered what the mills had failed to provide: the treatment of health problems.

Model apartments built by the Ahmedabad housing board for mill workers in the mid-1950s. In front a rally of the *Seva Dal*, a corps of volunteers used by Congress and TLA for crowd control in mass meetings.

Encouraging education was also high on the agenda. In 1924, 9 day schools for children and 11 evening schools for adults were opened, with a total of 1,200 registered pupils. The same year saw the publication of the first issue of *Majoor Sandesh,* a weekly newspaper produced on the TLA's own printing press. The paper, which is still published, informed workers about the union's aims, working methods, programmes and results. For its educational activities, which also included the opening of neighbourhood reading rooms, the union received an annual contribution from employers, not all of them though were in favour of this form of support. One is recorded as having expressed the fear that schooling would reduce the workers' interest in working at the mills. Despite all these efforts, a TLA survey of workers' families conducted in 1930 reported that barely one-fifth had any literate members. A cooperative savings society where members could acquire low-interest loans was set up to combat the high level of indebtedness to private moneylenders. In 1947, the union took a step further and set up its own bank, the only one of its kind in the country.

A shorter working day meant that, for the first time, the workers were able to do other things than just work to provide their daily necessities. The union instructed them in how they could spend their hours of leisure in useful pursuits rather than to fritter them away by gambling, drinking, or simply doing nothing. Gandhi and the prominent leaders of the union believed that the misery of the workers' living conditions was the result not so much of exploitation and oppression as of the inferior quality of life of those at the base of society, from which most of the union's members came. They could only hope for a better future if they were prepared to mend their ways.

Increasing knowledge was high on the union's agenda. Encouraging men to read was an important means of putting an end to their ignorance and their alleged lack of civic responsibility. The wives and daughters of mill workers learned to operate sewing machines so they could make and repair clothes for their families. Advocating piety, virtue and sobriety was founded on the significance attached by Gandhi to instilling into the working classes a higher moral standard than that to which they were accustomed. In 1928, the TLA announced the foundation of a social reform movement which called for total abstinence from alcohol and tobacco, and for other forms of self-discipline. The group singing of religious songs (*bhajan mandli*) in small informal gatherings became a popular pastime. In addition to purifying their souls, the workers were also encouraged to take better care of their bodies and, for the young in particular, to take part in sporting activities. The dozens of wrestling clubs (*akhadas*) attracted participants and spectators from a wide range of communities.

Sports were strictly the domain of men and exercises in the martial arts such as *kusti* (wrestling) became very popular.

धी મજૂર સહકારી બૅંક લી.
અમદાવાદ

Opening of the Labour Cooperative Bank which was housed in Anasuyaben's bungalow. Next to Shankarlal Banker in the centre are Khandubhai Desai and Shamprasad Vasavada. Navinchandra Barot, Arvind Buch and Manhar Shukla, leaders of the next generation, are also sitting in the front row.

Persistent communalism

Clearly, the social work also led to greater interaction and awareness among the working population. Away from the workplace, many meeting places developed where people from different backgrounds came together for educational or recreational purposes. This social part of the union's programme was important in itself, but also greatly increased the capacity of the workers to act collectively and to participate in clubs and associations.

Given the considerable importance attached to all kinds of social reforms, it is remarkable that there was no room on the union's agenda for measures aimed at breaking through the traditional caste system. The total failure to address the rigid hierarchical order was of course due to the fact that Gandhian teaching accepted caste and all it stood for as a focal unit in the structuring of society. Instead of rejecting the caste regime, therefore, the emphasis was on curbing its excesses and the intolerable practices of untouchability in particular. Efforts to this end were, however, feeble and the results meagre. The division of labour in the mills along lines of caste and religion was not questioned, while the communal pattern of housing was also sustained, with members of the untouchable castes segregated in separate residential blocks.

The weak support given by TLA leaders to those who supported the emancipation of the untouchables must be seen in the light of the resistance to such an outspoken policy in mainstream urban society. The rejection of caste reforms was shared by those members of the union who did not themselves belong to the ranks of the harijans. In the eyes of critics, the refusal to actively campaign for caste equality was a blemish on the mission that had been launched as the 'righteous struggle'. Muslim weavers showed

To repair broken threads or to suck yarn onto a new weft bobbin workers had to use their mouth. This was the main reason why dalits were confined to employment in the spinning departments.

their lack of faith in the union's economic and social agenda in a much more radical fashion and many of them refused to join. As we have already seen, the division along caste lines was also embedded in the structure of the union itself. This was a logical consequence of an acceptance, as a fact of life, of the link between occupation and social identity on the workfloor.

To lighten the burden for female employees, a law was introduced in 1922 forbidding them to work after seven o'clock in the evening and before 5.30 in the morning, while many mills offered young mothers the possibility of leaving their babies (but not toddlers) in crèches. As with the installation of

When many women were still employed in the mills creches were opened where they could leave their babies.

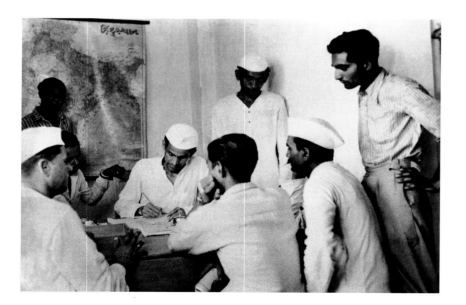

latrines and the ample provision of safe drinking water, these facilities were insisted upon as much with a view to increasing the dignity of labour as from a concern for the workers' health. For the same reason, employers were pressurised into opening canteens and permitting work to be interrupted by short but regular breaks. The steady expansion of legal protection kept pace with the progressive standardization of terms of employment in all the mills. This development marked the start of what would grow to become one of the most successful features of the union programme: the right of members to submit a complaint if they had suffered an injustice. The substantial staff of the TLA responsible for investigating grievances would take up such cases with the management of the company concerned; it also nominated its own representatives in the mills, who maintained direct contact with the union office. These were the *pratinidhis,* who functioned as shop stewards. They collected the membership fees on payday from the workers in their gang and took these to the union office, a task for which they were given a 5 per cent commission.

◀

Shantibhai Shah, in charge of the TLA section which dealt with grievances, filing a complaint.

More for the workers than by the workers

In the eyes of the mill owners, the change of course from confrontation to collaboration contributed strongly to the legitimacy of the union's work. In representing the interests of its members, the TLA's strategy was founded on what the Gandhian leadership saw as a sense of social responsibility. The prudent demands submitted to the employers and the welfare work undertaken in the industrial localities testified to reservations among the union leadership regarding the willingness of its members to lead a sober and diligent life. The union weekly urged the workers to behave as good employees – in other words to follow the orders of the management closely, perform their tasks with dedication, and avoid agitators, even if they were unable to get immediate and full justice. The appeal to behave reasonably also extended of course to acceptance of the TLA's goals and its chosen course . Employers showed themselves duly satisfied with this constructive ideology. The report of the Royal Commission on Labour in India (1931) summed up its opinion of the Gandhian variant of organized labour in Ahmedabad by saying that 'the union is managed more for than by the workers'. It is striking that in the long history of the Gandhian union not a single ordinary worker has ever been made a member of the executive board.

As the number of mills increased and the capacity of the spinning and weaving shops expanded, more workers were taken on. Encouraged by the high profits enjoyed by the mills in the second half of the 1920s, the union tabled a new demand, the right of labour to a family wage sufficient to cover the cost of living, in more senses than just that of survival. The city's captains of industry flatly rejected the demand, but Gandhi insisted that an employer was obliged to pay his workers at least a living wage right up to the moment that it was necessary for him to use his reserves for the company to remain in business. The economic crisis of the early 1930s also made itself felt in the textile industry in Ahmedabad. Unsold stocks expanded rapidly and a large number of companies found themselves with a cash-flow problem. In the second half of the decade, the economy began to recover, but industrial capacity would not return to its former level until 1939. The recession had, of course, a significant impact on the working population, a mass that had doubled in size between 1918 and 1930. The crisis reached its deepest point in 1933. A survey conducted at the end of the year revealed that more than half of the weavers and a quarter of the spinners had lost their jobs. When the employers' union announced a 25 per cent wage cut, the TLA responded by insisting on the right of its members to earn enough for their family's livelihood. A clash was avoided at the last minute, firstly because the TLA, as always, was prepared to reach a compromise, but also because the employers realized that erosion of the union's power would invoke an even greater threat – that it would no longer be possible to settle the unrest among the industrial vanguard of the working masses by Gandhian means. The dispute went to arbitration, and the result was a considerably lower wage cut than earlier proposed, but the union had to agree to rationalization of the operations in the mills to increase productivity. Women in particular were dismissed in large numbers. In the early years of the textile industry, women had made up 15 to 20 per cent of the workforce, but this proportion was now much lower. Men were given priority as the natural candidates for jobs in the formal sector of the economy. This exclusion of women from work in the mills was in accordance with Gandhi's belief that their natural role was as wives and mothers at home.

**Members of TLA's Executive Board, all of them of non-working class vintage,
in the early 1950s; in the centre the General Secretary Shamaprasad Vasavada.**

Shiv Shankar Shukla as coordinator of womens's activities shortly before Elaben Bhatt took over in the mid 1950s.

When Elaben Bhatt joined the TLA Navinchandra Barot was her boss.

Male and female workers cast their vote for *pratinidhi* elections near Ashok mill.

▶

Training workshop for *pratinidhis* in the main hall of the TLA office with Manhar Shukla sitting in the centre.

Gandhi was the most important politician in shaping the labour movement of Ahmedabad. A huge crowd turned up to pay their last respects when his ashes were immersed in the Sabarmati river after his assassination in 1948.

Sardar Patel, who kept his distance from the industrial working class, addressed only a few weeks before his death in 1950 a TLA meeting on Labour Day *(Majoor Din)*.This function is annually held on December 4th to commemorate the beginning of the strike in 1918.

In the mill localities Indulal Yagnik was undoubtedly the most popular of the three political leaders.

▶

Rally held at the time of the Maha Gujarat movement in 1955-56. By then the bicycle had become part of the formal attire of male mill workers.

Ongoing expansion

After the rationalization of the crisis years, the textile industry entered a new period of expansion. The Second World War put a stop to imports from abroad, giving production, for the domestic market and for military equipment, a considerable boost. The industry's position was further strengthened after Independence, when the government adopted a protectionist economic policy.

Growth of the textile industry 1861-1939				
Year	Mills	Spindles	Looms	Workers
1861	1	2,500	-	63
1881	9	193,737	2,485	2,013
1905	32	577,166	7,197	16,964
1918	51	1,061,115	22,255	35,415
1921	53	1,088,820	23,208	43,515
1931	76	1,743,523	40,022	69,562
1939	77	1,901,872	46,853	77,859

The number of mills in Ahmedabad fell in later years, but spinning and weaving capacity expanded. This, together with the fact that many mills lengthened the chain of production by opening their own printing and dyeing departments, led to substantial growth in employment in the industry. At the end of the 1970s, the city had a little over 60 corporate mills, employing a total of almost 160,000 workers.

The End of Mill Production

The persistent demand for more labour in the mid 20th century provoked a new wave of immigration, this time from further afield. Among those who flocked to join the industrial vanguard in Ahmedabad were Kanbi Patels from the north and west of Gujarat, Muslims from Uttar Pradesh and members of the lower castes from Andhra Pradesh and Maharasthra. Their arrival was one of the major factors contributing to the growth in the city's population.

At the same time, in the wider metropolitan economy, there were the first signs of a shift towards the informal sector. The textile mills no longer determined the face of the urban landscape or constituted the primary source of income for working class households in the city. Between 1971 and 1981, the total population of Ahmedabad grew from 1.75 to 2.59 million, a tenfold increase since the beginning of the century. As it grew, the proportion of people employed in the formal sector declined progressively. In 1981, of a working population of three-quarters of a million, half a million depended for their basic needs on the informal sector. In the early 1970s, 150,000 of the 250,000 formal sector workers in the city were still registered as industrial labourers, the majority employed by the corporate textile enterprises. In subsequent years their numbers fell steeply and by the end of the century no more than 20,000 of the previous formidable army were still left. With the closure of more and more mills, the sacked workers found themselves forced to the bottom of the urban economy. I shall return later to this downturn in their fortunes and how it affected their lives. The emphasis here is on what the members of the industrial vanguard in Ahmedabad achieved during their struggle to improve their lot in the good years preceding the mill closures.

The blow room is the first phase of the cotton production process and is followed by spinning, weaving, dyeing, printing, folding, and packing.

The shrinking number of women still employed in the spinning
departments were on retirement replaced by young males.

Machines had become bigger as well as more complicated
and required operators with better skills than before.

 Workers at the end of the production line were usually from higher castes. They did not take off their pants and shirts as was the custom among the low-caste workforce employed in the overheated and humid halls in the early stages of production.

A labour aristocracy

One of the most important factors that distinguished the mill workers from the unorganized mass in the informal sector of the economy was membership of a trade union. The industrial legislation from the late colonial period permitted unions to take part in regular consultations with employers and the government only if they represented at least a quarter of the workers in their sector of industry. This restriction reinforced the TLA's leading position in the labour movement in Ahmedabad. Because they were excluded from the negotiations on wages and terms, other unions with a more radical agenda had no opportunity to expand. In the decades that followed, membership of the Gandhian union increased as never before. Until the end of the 1970s, the TLA represented three in every four workers in the city's textile industry, an extraordinarily high level of organization. Can this also be seen as an indication of the members' unconditional support and trust in the union leadership?

Without a doubt, the TLA succeeded in achieving significant improvements in the working and living conditions of its members. The working day was reduced to eight hours. Child labour was banned. The level of education rose and, although the workers received no formal training, the increasing complexity of the machines they had to operate meant that they became more and more skilled. Facilities such as drinking water, toilets, and canteens upgraded the quality of the working environment. Although the workplace continued to be dirty, dangerous, and unhealthy, the mills were not as bad as they had been previously. And the bosses treated those in their charge less brutally. The regime on the workfloor was still very strict, but the violence was verbal rather than physical. One sign that times had changed was that

now employees could – and did – complain. The gap between incomes from work in the bazar economy and those in the mills had grown ever larger. Not only were the mill hands better paid, they also had a right to a range of bonuses, including a dearness allowance, an extra month's salary a year, and even an allowance for coming to work on their bicycles. Employers tried to prevent the introduction of an annual bonus because they said it would only increase absenteeism and the extra income would be spent on drink. But they were unable to halt the improvements in the quality of the workers' lives. These favourable terms of employment also had a visible effect on the workers' living environment. The labour legislation included provisions to protect them against premature dismissal and health insurance covered the medical costs of both the workers and members of their households. On retirement they received a benefit from the Providence Fund. Clearly, between the start of the 20th century and the 1970s, great advances were made in dignifying industrial labour.

Given these positive results of the 'righteous struggle', it is striking to note that the TLA members by no means adopted a subservient attitude to the union leaders. The extent to which that they were prepared to depart from the course set out by the union first became apparent in the 1950s, when the workers gave their enthusiastic support to Indulal Yagnik, a populist politican and fierce opponent of the TLA. Again at the end of the 1960s, during the break with the Congress Party, the TLA members sided *en masse* with Indira Gandhi, to the great displeasure of the Gandhian leadership. This contrary attitude must be understood against the background of the paternalistic authoritarian style that the TLA bosses, most of whom belonged to the bourgeoisie, had adopted from the very beginning.

New hands were trained on the job, usually by their relatives or caste-mates.

Over time basic facilities had somewhat improved. Most mills provided drinking water, had urinals and a canteen, but the sites of work remained extremely grim and ugly places to be.

Even in the early 1980s a nail on the wall was all the workers had to hang their clothes on.

Failing industrial entrepreneurship

What were the causes of the closures of most of the textile mills in Ahmedabad in the final quarter of the 20th century? Some factors that played a part will be examined in the following chapter. Before moving on, however, it must first be made clear that the mill owners did more to help bring about the downfall of the industry than they did to prevent it. During the many years of prosperity in the middle of the century, they failed to reinvest their excessive profits in modern technology and more efficient management. Factory buildings and machinery became obsolete and worn out. With management paying absolutely no attention to training or a decent labour policy, productivity stagnated. The often-heard claim that inefficiency on the workfloor was the result of the low quality and lack of commitment of the workforce confused cause and effect. The Gandhian ideal of an alliance between labour and capital faltered not so much because of the refusal of the industrial vanguard to play by the rules; of much greater significance was the steadfast unwillingness of the employers, from beginning to end, to allow their employees a fair share in the industry's profits.

The high tariffs with which the nationalist leaders protected domestic industries against foreign competition in the first decades after Independence meant that the textile magnates in Ahmedebad received a very high return on their capital, which they had often been given by the state as loans on very favourable terms. Instead of using these earnings to introduce crucial innovations to prepare their companies for a globalized economy based on free trade, they chose to invest in other areas of industrial and non-industrial activity where market prospects were more favourable. This was partly due to the mercantile background of the prominent families in the city. Their reputations as renowned 'captains of industry' concealed their original identities as traders and moneylenders. They had never been industrialists in the real sense of the word. Their lack of the innovative and future-oriented qualities that are inherent to entrepreneurship explain why, when their careers as industrial magnates came to such a bitter end, they paid so little attention to the miserable fate of those who had been in their employ.

Spindle repair; members of the technical staff often did not have a seperate workshop for repairs but went around the various departments with their simple tools.

Buildings and compounds were covered with grime
and soot. Dyeing added to the industrial pollution.

Cotton dust was the cause of bysinosis, a fatal disease
which employers chose to ignore and from which many
mill workers must have died already at an early age.

The final drama

The wave of mill closures which swept through the city in the last quarter of the 20th century came as a great shock to the workers. Even for those who had lost their jobs in the first round of closures during the late seventies, the memory of this turning point in their lives continues to invoke deep emotions. The mill sirens were a familiar and regular sound in industrial localities. At the change of shift the air would be filled with noise as each mill signalled to its employees to end or start their daily work. While reflecting on the good old days, one former mill worker wistfully tole of how the sound had always reminded him of mothers calling their children playing in the streets to come home.

But was dismissal really a bolt from the blue? That is very unlikely, particularly in the later years. After all, many others had suffered the same fate before. In most cases the writing had been on the wall for their own mill for a long time. Recurrent losses interrupted the regular flow of production and suppliers were only prepared to deliver raw materials on a cash basis. Workers were often sent home for days or weeks on end because there was nothing for them to do, and were told there was no money to pay their wages. Vacancies as a result of retirement or failing health were no longer filled, the third shift was discontinued, and whole departments were closed for an unspecified period. These measures were obviously a cause for concern but, since such interruptions or reductions had been regular events during the 1960s and 1970s, it was perhaps understandable that it still came as a surprise to many when production stopped for good.

Closure

The final curtain fell when the electricity was cut off because the bill had not been paid, or when a creditor had the mill declared bankrupt. In either case, it would be the owner himself who provoked this intervention to evade his legal duty to give prior notice of his intention to close the mill. His standard reaction was that he had not made the decision of his own free will. By claiming *force majeure* he could defend himself against accusations of not having fulfilled his statutory obligations. These included, primarily, a fair redundancy scheme based on years of service, and other compensations for the now superfluous workforce. By the time the mill closed, the owner had already withdrawn the capital he had invested in the enterprise in the preceding years. In many cases, the management also tried to transfer the mill records elsewhere, take away any remaining stock and raw materials, and dismantle the looms and other machines to be sold for scrap. For their part, the alarmed workers tried to prevent these secretive and illegal practices by picketing the mill gates and searching all vehicles.

Writing the bad news to the family back at home in North India.

Sharing the blame

Apart from the bad faith of many owners, there were other factors which contributed to the collapse of large-scale enterprises. One was the progressive switch from cotton production to synthetic yarns as a result of new dress fashions among consumers. In addition to loss of competitiveness due to low productivity, for which failing management practices were mainly responsible, the weaving shops of the composite mills in particular had lost their viability. While in several companies the spinning department remained open, other departments stopped processing the yarn produced. Weaving was relocated to small and low-cost workshops on the city's outskirts, with no protection at all for the workers involved. These dramatic changes in the organization of production took place in the context of a new government policy on the textile industry that was introduced in 1985 and which gave priority to economic liberalization and the flexibilization of labour relations. It basically meant privileging small-scale manufacture, in powerloom sheds that had sprung up in the informal sector of the economy, above large-scale production, in composite mills in the formal sector of the economy. Much more could be said about the restructuring of industrial capital that has taken place in recent decades but our concern here is with the massive retrenchment of the army of mill workers and with the dramatic changes that this has brought about in their way of life.

The sharp decline of large-scale textile production did not occur only in Ahmedabad, but nowhere else in India did it have such a deep impact. During the first round of closures in the late 1970s and early 1980s, 40,000 labourers lost their secure jobs. The new industrial policy in 1985 gave rise to a second and even more substantial round of closure and retrenchment.

Towards the end of the last decade of the 20th century, 52 enterprises had ceased operating or were on the verge of locking the mill gates. In late 1996 the workforce had shrunk to not more than 25,000. Updated figures on the army of rejected mill workers are hard to come by, but their number further increased in the final years of the 20th century. The famous Calico mill, one of the oldest enterprises owned by the Sarabhai family, closed down and the huge Reliance company laid off a large segment of its workforce in 2001.

Pratinidhi **urging workers to attend a protest meeting.**

Workers discussing amongst themselves how to put pressure on
management and government to reopen their mill.

Protest

The dismissed workers had good reason for holding the mill owners primarily responsible for their ill fortune. The employers had discovered that it was cheaper to wind up their companies and transfer production to small-scale workshops where they did not have to comply with labour legislation. They also went in search of new and more profitable business endeavours in other industries or sectors of the economy to invest their capital. Although the closures were a direct result of a strategy to aquire cheap labour, neither the government nor the trade union opposed the transfer of production away from the mills. The union officials were, therefore, docile accessories to the mass redundancies.

The resentment and anger of the retrenched workers against those who should have represented their interests at the critical conjuncture is fully understandable. After all, more than any other organization, the TLA claimed to have fought incessantly to improve the lot of the working masses in the cotton mills. Moreover, it was the only union authorized to negotiate with the employers on terms of employment. The top-down policy to which the union bosses adhered right to the end had shaped the TLA's operational style from the very beginning. The General Secretary was appointed thirty years ago, and the other senior board members have been there just as long. Their authoritarian leadership leaves no room for accountability or even the minimum of genuine participation by members in appointing, promoting, or dismissing union officials. The ideological choice to avoid militancy in favour of harmony and cooperation with the captains of industry, as well as the choice of compromise as the basic principle of settling disputes, explains the detachment and the indifference with which the TLA responded to the

◀ ▲

Workers rally in 1984 : "Reopen 'Silver cotton'! ", "Reopen
the shut mills! Long live the workers' unity!"

mass exodus of nine-tenths of its members during the ongoing crisis in the textile industry. The stories told by many ex-mill workers express in clear terms their feelings of disillusionment and bitterness about the refusal of the veteran stalwarts of the union to make a more decisive stand to prevent the redundancies.

Did the union take no action at all? In response to the closures in the early 1980s, instant protest meetings were staged when the owner of a company announced that the gates were going to be shut, this time forever. Marches through the city's centre attracted great public attention. Politicians and various agencies of the state government were called upon in no uncertain terms to intervene. As the years passed and it became clear that the entire branch of industry was in a deep and even terminal crisis, the earlier clamour which resonated throughout the city dissipated. Whereas the initial closures had generated great indignation in Ahmedabad, public sympathy gradually waned. The municipal authorities were quick to defuse all signs of restiveness. In the 1990s each new case of bankruptcy and the ensuing loss of many hundreds or even thousands of jobs invoked little response outside the immediate circle of victims. Media reports were restricted to the bare facts and mainstream politicians seemed to have lost their earlier interest in the issue.

This protest march ended at the statue of Indulal Yagnik who was a staunch critic, in the 1950s and 1960s, of both the captains of industry and the leadership of the Gandhian trade union.

The wall graffiti reads : "Closed mill workers and the educated unemployed, let's all go to Gandhinagar - 23-6-1984"

The promise of industrial renovation

And yet there was still hope for a return to better times. In the 1970s, within the framework of the centrally regulated economy, the state and its agencies showed themselves willing to prevent the shutdown of 'sick' private industries by transferring them to the public sector . The strategy was to inject new capital and to rationalize production, so that companies could continue as viable concerns with a smaller but more efficient workforce. To implement this policy the National Textile Corporation (NTC) was established in 1974 and ample funds were allocated to improve management and to cut down on labour costs. In 1986, the Gujarat State Textile Corporation (GSTC) was launched with a mandate to restructure 12 closed corporate mills into 5 or 6 revitalized enterprises. Both agencies utterly failed in their primary objective: to save at least some of the jobs lost through technological and operational modernization. But the workers eventually brought under the public sector regime at least had their redundancy rights intact. They received all their back pay, the money they had built up in the Provident Fund and a retrenchment allowance based on their years of service. The workers in mills threatened with closure therefore hoped that the companies would be taken over by the NTC or GSTC. They might lose their jobs, but they would at least be assured of receiving the savings and other dues. In the final years of the 20th century the NTC was in charge of 12 sick mills, which formerly employed 23,200 workers, more than half of whom had been railroaded into taking advantage of the voluntary redundancy scheme. The remaining 10,400 received what was called 'idle wages': although production had come to a halt, the workers still on the books continued to be paid, albeit irregularly and not fully.

While weaving had stopped, spinning continued in several mills, although at reduced capacity.

The industrial economy which, since Independence, had been largely based on central planning and control gradually made way for a policy in which production and sales were increasingly determined by the free market. This turnaround, which peaked in 1991, was followed a year later by the setting up of a National Renewal Fund (NRF). The aim of the fund was to cover the costs of benefits for workers who had become superfluous in certain branches of industry, such as textiles, to pay for their retraining, and to finance the creation of new jobs. However, the largest part of the budget for the fund was spent on the voluntary redundancy of workers in mills that had been taken over by the government. But, even among them, the programme was not received with great enthusiasm. What had been proclaimed as a social safety net was seen by the recipients as meagre compensation for the loss of their protected right to income from regular employment. Yet the few tens of thousands of workers in Ahmedabad who were eligible for these state redundancy schemes were in an enviable position. The many more who had worked in mills that had remained in private hands until closure not only received no compensation at all for their redundancy – which should have been equal to a sliding scale from between 75 per cent of their last salary initially to 25 per cent at the end for a three-year period – but were often dismissed without even being paid the full amount that was owed to them for as long as they had worked. Statistics show that 72,840 permanent workers at 46 mills did not receive their statutory dues, which averaged 31,293 rupees per worker. While the majority received nothing, a minority was paid part or all of their various compensations. Such unequal treatment made the shock of dismissal even more intense. The amount of redundancy pay was in no way related to their service record. A happy few were 'lucky' and received what they were entitled to, but many more who were unlucky enough not to be dismissed in the last instance by the government got little or nothing at all.

▲ ▶

Several private enterprises which had gone bankrupt were given a new lease of life in the public sector. Awaiting their revitalization with new management and equipment, these workers were not dismissed and received what was called empty wages. Their daily presence was required to pass muster, so that they may enter their names in the register of attendance.

Cheated out of compensation

The TLA leadership took steps to ensure that its members received all the money owed to them and full redundancy pay by threatening to take defaulting owners to court. This was a slow and costly process that usually ended, if at all, with a settlement and payment of a much lower sum than had been claimed. The costs of legal assistance had to be covered from the meagre fruits of this victory. Rumours were rife in the textile districts that union leaders were in cahoots with the bosses and were putting part of the redundancy money into their own pockets. These suspicions were fuelled by the fact that the TLA asked for a fee to finance disputes with the employers, in order to pay the lawyers hired. This commission – 1 per cent of the final payment – was the cause of much controversy and, according to one calculation, earned the union some 165 lakhs rupees.

The flexibilization of the labour market that accompanied the policy of deregulation meant that employment was no longer governed by the industrial legislation put in place in the years before and after Independence. The impact on the dismissed labour force in Ahmedabad will be dealt with later. Here the focus is on the government's steadfast refusal to ensure compliance with the body of legal provisions that safeguarded the rights of the workers up to the time that they were dismissed. State agencies systematically failed to exercise political, administrative, and legal pressure on the mill owners to fulfil their obligations towards their employees. Despite the malefide and fraudulent manner in which most of the closures took place, there were almost no cases of captains of industry being prosecuted by the state, let alone their being punished for their illegal actions.

Manhar Shukla, still General Secretary in the dying days of the TLA.

Takeover by the NTC or GSTC was a precondition for the success of workers' claims against reluctant employers. The chances of this happening were greater in the early years of closure. Workers who were lucky enough to gain public employee status before losing their jobs could count on a redundancy payment from the NRF. But even then, and contrary to earlier promises, the majority of them did not receive the full amount they were owed. This privilege was restricted to managerial staff members, whose exit was often accompanied by a golden handshake. The lower one's position in the hierarchy, the greater the chance of being put out on the street with little or nothing. The excessive inequality in the treatment of dismissed workers, both between and within companies, considerably intensified the misery resulting from the loss of job and livelihood. The General Secretary of the TLA told us during a conversation at the end of 1999 that the former mill workers had altogether received no more than a fifth of the total compensation and other payments to which they were entitled. The righteous struggle had ended in dismal failure.

At the time of closure union members came to the TLA office to hear the latest news and to fill up forms for their claim to compensation.

A peacock perching above looms which have been silent for many years.

Profile of ex-mill workers

What was the stock of social capital represented by the dismissed textile workers, and what has happened to these people and to the households of which they were the main, and often only, providers? In 1998 I conducted a survey, together with Dr B.B. Patel, professor at the Gandhian Labour Institute in Ahmedabad, among 600 ex-mill workers living in the industrial districts around the old city and who became unemployed between the early 1980s and the late 1990s. We collected data on their origin, gender, age, literacy, and communal identity, as well as on their former skills and income, together with other benefits they used to derive from mill employment. The results of the survey are summarized below.

Four-fifths of the dismissed workers originate from Gujarat. Three-fifths were born in Ahmedabad or have lived in the city since early childhood. These figures confirm that the majority of the mill workers had strong ties with the city. Family histories show that grandfathers and great-grandfathers were recruited from nearby districts. Ties with the village of origin have hardly survived. Around the middle of the 20th century many more migrants settled in the city. They were landpoor or landless peasants driven from their rural habitat as far away as Uttar Pradesh, Rajasthan, Maharashtra, and Andhra Pradesh to seek a better future in the mills of Ahmedabad. In most cases, their status as newcomers has become diluted after several decades in the city. Most of them refused to leave the city after the mills were shut because of the lack of employment 'at home' and because their children are so used to life in the city that they would not be able to resettle in the countryside.

Falling through the safety net

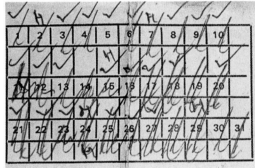

The job has gone but most workers have retained their mill card as a precious relic of a lost identity.

▶

Harish Pasawala belongs to the (high) Soni caste and used to be employed in the engineering department on a good salary. When his mill closed in 1995 he received the compensation money to which he was entitled (Rs. 70,000). He then started manufacturing fans but had to give up this business because of lack of capital. Now he is employed only as a badli (substitute) in the Ashima mill earning Rs.148 on days of employment. His son works as a computer operator, also in the Ashima mill, at a monthly wage of Rs. 2,500.

With the exception of a tiny fraction of two to three per cent women, the workers in the cotton mills were men. The dramatic reversal in the fortunes of the dismissed workers came at the peak of their working lives. There were not many below 25 years of age. The mill management saw the crisis coming for a long time and failed to replace older employees with younger ones as they retired. More than half of those who lost their jobs were between 25 and 44. Thus, the average ex-mill worker was a male with quite a few years of service but with many still to go before retiring.

Nine out of ten males were married and lived together with their wife and children. Four-fifths were the heads of their households; the rest were sons or brothers, while the few females were wives, mothers, or daughters. Although the first few generations of mill workers were still illiterate, this percentage fell rapidly as the 20th century progressed; over time only 15 per cent were unable to read and write. A fifth completed half of their primary education and nearly one third had a primary school certificate. This means that even among the least educated more than half enjoyed some basic schooling.

The ex-mill workforce can be divided into four categories. Slightly more than one - third are members from scheduled castes who nowadays call themselves *dalits*. Predominant among them are Vankars and Chamars, castes which were previously known in rural Gujarat as weavers and leather workers respectively. The 'other backward castes' (known as OBCs) consist of a wide range of castes, especially Thakors and Vaghris. The middle castes include Sonis, Rajputs, Darbars, and Jats, but the largest caste is that of the Patels, which outnumber all of these together. The Muslims, too, are not a homogeneous community but are divided into a number of caste-like groups.

Most of the lower ranks in the mill hierarchy were trained on the job. Newcomers were in effect assigned tasks according to their social identity: spinning, weaving, or working in one of the departments where the textiles were processed further. A worker became skilled overed several months by learning from an experienced workmate. This was usually a family or caste member, quite often the same person who had helped the workers get the job in the first place. Getting a regular job at a mill was a tedious and lengthy process. The first stage was to register as a reserve worker or badli. This meant reporting for work every day but only actually working in the absence of one of the regular members of the shift. It was quite common for workers to try and get a temporary pass in more than one mill. To be considered for a permanent job, candidates had to turn up day in and day out, and even then, they only succeeded with the help of someone on the inside. As a consequence of the close correlation between social identity and work in the mill, the segmentation between the various departments closely reflected the pattern of communal segregation. The division along caste and religious lines was further accentuated by a hierarchical structure which paralleled the finely graded stratification in wider society: a very broad base where Dalit castes, Baxi Panches and Muslims lived and worked in close proximity, with a smaller segment above comprising members of the middle and higher castes who were engaged in 'cleaner' and more respected work.

The wages in the cotton mills were standardized on the basis of an agreed minimum, a dearness allowance, and an annual bonus. Until the early 1980s, textile workers were among the best paid industrial workers in India. The crisis which swept through the whole country from the late 1970s, and which caused such a dramatic decrease in the number of people working in the textile industry, did not merely result in a fall in real incomes but also

Ex-mill hand re-employed in a powerloom workshop on informal sector conditions.
He has a casual rather than a regular contract, works longer hours, has no holidays
or health insurance, and is paid a much lower, piece rate wage.

wiped out the lead this sector had previously enjoyed in employment conditions. Within a comparatively short time, wages were lagging behind those in other branches of heavy industry, such as metal and machine manufacture. Nevertheless, right up to the time that the mills closed, the textile workers enjoyed a much better standard of living than the large majority of the labouring classes in Ahmedabad, who had to survive outside the formal sector of the economy. This gap was not only a matter of actual earnings per day, week, or month. The mill workers and their families were also entitled to a whole range of low-cost or free provisions, including medical insurance, sick pay, paid leave, a Provident Fund to which the employer contributed half of the premium and which was used to finance the workers' pension, and access to cheap credit from the mill's own credit bank to help cover major expenses. Lastly, the employer sometimes provided some workers with free or low-rent accommodation, usually in the immediate vicinity of the mill.

The terms of employment of textile workers with permanent jobs in the cotton mills were backed up by industrial legislation and became part of an institutional framework for consultation in which government bodies and employers' and employees' organizations participated. The acceptance of these tripartite procedures for negotiating the interests of the protected segment of the working class had much to do with the advent of the trade union movement. Acknowledging the need for representation, most mill workers in Ahmedabad were members of the TLA right up to the day they lost their jobs.

The owners of the new processing units do not have to bother about labour rights and the safety regulations prescribed by the Factory Act.

Retraining the sacked workforce

The National Renewal Fund launched in 1992 as part of the new economic policy was proclaimed to be a social safety net. In addition to paying out compensation it was also to be used to retrain the dismissed mill workers and help them re-enter the labour market. As we have seen, the pledge to provide compensation for the jobs lost was broken on a massive scale. So what became of the other part of the state-sponsored rehabilitation scheme, launched with much fanfare? As a matter of fact, what was eventually spent on retraining programmes was only a minor fraction of the already meagre budget earmarked for this purpose.

Employee Resource Centres were opened in the mill localities of Ahmedabad, where the workers could apply for retraining and obtain advice on how best to make use of their redundancy payments (when and if they received them). It proved, however, difficult to interest the workers in these activities. Between 1994, when the retraining programme started, and 1998 no more than 7,000 former mill workers took part, much fewer than had been expected. This was partly due to the criteria imposed for admission. The programme was open only to men who could prove that they had a permanent job at the time of closure (thereby disqualifying, in advance, women, badli workers, and regular employees who had opted for voluntary retirement before theirs mills were shut down), who were younger than 55 at the time they registered for the programme, and who had at least completed their primary education. Nevertheless, the majority of the dismissed workers fulfilled these criteria. So why did they not register for the programme in much greater numbers?

▲▼
These men were pressurised in April 2001 to give up their jobs with Reliance, one of the largest corporate textile mills in Ahmedabad, under the so-called Voluntary Retirement Scheme with the threat that those unwilling to comply would risk losing their redundancy pay.

Announcements in newspapers and posters in the Labour Welfare Centres disseminated information on this part of the safety net. The main reason for the lukewarm response was a lack of confidence among the sacked workers in the practical value of the promises made. Their sceptical or downright hostile response turned out to be well founded. The courses on offer promised training for technical occupations, such as those of an electrician, tailor, carpenter, plumber, motor mechanic, radio repairman, and diamond polisher. It was also possible to enlist for driving lessons. The courses were given by qualified instructors, usually in vocational or industrial training centres. The training given was, however, much too short. It lasted for fifty days at the most, spread over two to three months. Candidates had no say in which new occupation they were to receive training. They were assigned to courses not according to their own preference but on the basis of where there were still vacancies. There was little protest against this callous handling of applications because many only signed up to receive the daily allowance of 40 rupees and did not bother to attend the lessons. Their instructors did not report their absence because they would lose out on the 9,000 rupees per head in course fees.

The reservations with which the unemployed workers viewed the utility of whatever they were taught was primarily founded on the absence of any guarantee that they would be able to practice what they had learnt. With its new economic policy of liberalization taking shape the government was neither able nor willing to bear any responsibility for creating new jobs. Three-quarters of the selected workers who took part in training courses did not find work in their new occupations. In addition to the complete lack of any counselling on where and how to find a job, most participants were not furnished with the basic tools required to practice their new skills. Although

1,800 rupees had been set aside for the purchase of a toolbox (such as a sewing machine for tailors, or a set of tools for carpenters and motor mechanics) on the successful completion of the course, in many cases these were not provided. All things considered, it is not surprising that interest in the courses dropped before industrial retraining was phased out altogether in 2000. It is difficult to avoid the impression that the decision to introduce the rehabilitation scheme was motivated more by a desire on the part of the government and politicians to make a show of support at a time when public opinion was still quite sensitive to the problem of mass redundancies, than by an honest and resolute attempt to 'recycle' the lost labour expelled from the cotton mills.

Last day of training at ITI Saraspur on 21 January 2002. The last salary of these men, dismissed from the Reliance company in the preceding year, was Rs. 3,800 to 4,000 per month. They are quite pessimistic about job prospects in their new line of training. Even if they succeed in finding new employment, they know that their daily income will be less than half of what they used to earn.

Bhikhabhai Naranbhai Parmar, Shankarbhai Jivabhai Patel and Govind Becharbhai Parmar, former workers at the Star of Gujarat and the Raipur mill, learn tailoring work in a course of three months. For setting up their own businesses, they will need at least a sewing machine but they have just been informed that none will be given.

The drive towards self-employment

What was presented as a social safety net was expressly intended to prepare the former mill workers to work – in contrast to their previous status as permanent waged labour – at their own risk and expense. A few of the training courses taught not particular occupational skills but gave instruction on how to start a micro-enterprise. The promotion of small-scale business also included the advocacy of modest bank loans to provide seed capital. Very few applications were actually granted and even then – after a procedure that took nearly one and a half years – only half the amount of money requested. Completely in line with this meagre result was the information provided by a government official at a meeting we attended to mark the end of a course to train former mill workers to be rickshaw drivers. After the speeches, the participants were asked if they had anything to say. There was only one question: how were they to get the money – 75,000 rupees – to buy an auto-rickshaw? The reply that they could apply for a bank loan was accompanied by a veiled warning that, without sufficient security, they stood no chance of acquiring one. Information leaflets gave the impression that it was easy to get loans, but the former textile workers knew better. Most of them had such a low level of solvency that they were refused on these grounds alone. Those who stuck it out long enough to finally become eligible for a loan were charged all manner of costs that never appeared in the official accounts. It often happened that they had to sign for a much higher amount than they actually got. Other 'donations' they were forced to make to middlemen in the long trajectory from application to approval of the loan made it much more expensive than it was on paper.

By establishing the transition from permanent waged employment to working at one's own risk and expense as the norm, the government displayed a disturbing lack of insight into what this change meant for the unemployed textile workers. Politicians and bureaucrats saw micro-enterprise as the driving force of a new existence for these workers in the informal sector of the urban economy. Without even the minimum capital and know-how, the victims of the closures were sent out onto the streets to earn a living as petty commodity producers. That only a few eventually chose this option was not difficult to foresee. Yet the fiction of self-employment is preserved in the pretence that those who work as casual labourers chose to do so. The reality is that the majority are by no means their own bosses and would much prefer regular and waged employment to being forced to perform all kinds of casual jobs to make ends meet. Work at one's own account also requires means of production and other forms of capital which the majority of workers do not have and cannot afford with the small budgets at their disposal: the purchase

Samsuddin Saiyad lost his job from New Gujarat Cotton mill where he was working in the printing department. He now drives a rikshaw and also leads the prayers at Vaaju-Saiyad Baba's *dargah* (a muslim shrine).

of equipment such as a sewing machine, a simple stall for pressing clothes or repairing shoes, a handcart to sell vegetables or drinks, a cycle or cart to deliver goods, money to pay for a driving licence or for a permit to sell kerosene. In addition to all that they need cash for *hafta*, the bribes paid to a policeman, a wholesale trader, or anyone else with power over the arena in which workers in the informal sector practise their trade or craft. The majority of former mill workers stubbornly ignore the wishful thinking of the policy makers and continue to look for waged employment. In the absence of permanent work, they have to settle for casual labour. Our conclusion is that neither industrial retraining nor any other weak attempts at state-sponsored rehabilitation have effected a turn for the better after the dramatic and sudden decline in the quality of the working life of the former mill workers.

One possible explanation for the waning public interest in the mill closures is that they were not caused by a more general crisis in the city's economy. The collapse of the corporate textile enterprises was accompanied by the rise of other industrial activity, such as petrochemical and pharmaceutical enterprises, cement factories, diamond cutting and polishing workshops, powerloom units, and garment ateliers. Even more important than the emergence of new industrial ventures was the shift in the city's economic balance to trade and services. By 1991 the population of greater Ahmedabad had risen to 3.3 million, of which a little over a million made up the workforce. But even more significant than this restructuring of economic activity in the city was the progressive loss of formal sector employment. Having been pushed out of their secure and protected jobs in the mills, the dismissed workers slid down into the already overcrowded informal sector of the economy.

The difference between these two shopkeepers is that Jivan Jayantilal Parmar(top) received compensation when his mill closed, while Khushalbhai Ganeshbhai Chauhan (bottom) received nothing.

Harikumar Yadav, originally from U.P., purchases metal waste from women. He started this business, together with his brother (sitting in the background), when they lost their mill jobs eight years ago. They invested their compensation money of Rs. 30,000 in this joint venture, which has turned out to be quite successful, yielding a monthly income of Rs. 3,500 for each of them.

Many street-based operators have no, or hardly any assets with which to increase the price for their labour power.

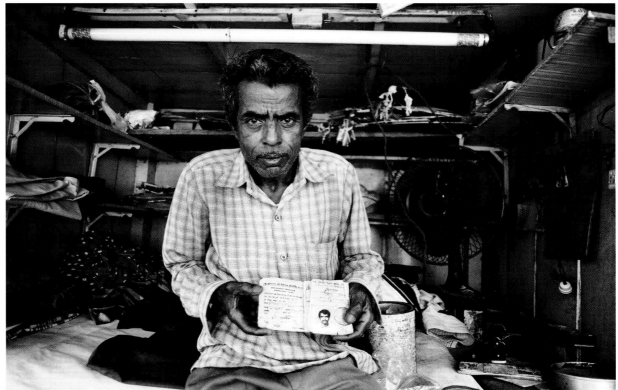

Madhavbhai Bakaram Ninde (59) came from Maharashtra in 1963 in search of a job. When his mill shut down in 1987 he found employment in powerloom workshops for fourteen years, but stopped because the wage was too low. For the past year, he has been moving around with a handcart selling vegetables. In addition to his own earnings of Rs. 1,200 per month, his first son brings home Rs. 1,500 from an embroidery workshop and his daughter-in-law has just found a job for a few hours each day as a housemaid.

Kalyanbhai Vankar (46) owns a tea stall in Amraiwadi. His mill was closed in 1984 and the period of unemployment which then followed, although many years ago, is still vivid in his mind: 'We survived on only tea-bread for three months'. Now he can maintain his household of six members because his eldest son, casually employed in a factory, contributes to the total income of Rs. 4,500 a month. Being unable to save anything at all from this amount, he worries about the future prospects of his children because they cannot be properly educated.

A TLA official took money from Rasul Gulam, who is now a petty shopkeeper in Sanklit Nagar, for filing his claim to compensation. But until today he has received nothing at all.

Repairing plastic buckets is employment of the last resort. This man's craft is only in demand because of the poverty of his customers.

Since his mill closed in 1994 Utbuddin Noormohammed has been a street vendor who collects scrap iron which he barters for popcorn. Out of eight members in his household, three are too young to work but all the others have to help in generating income.

Muslim labourers preparing sevainya, a food product which is an important ingredient in the daily meals of their community.

The pain of adjustment

For the former mill workers, their initial refusal to accept that the mills had closed for good was replaced by a realization that there was no other option than to look for work elsewhere. Some of them adapted to this dramatic change in their living conditions relatively quickly while others were slower sometimes taking several months to orient themselves to a different way of making a living. The main factors determining response were age and level of education or training. The older workers found it more difficult to say farewell to life in the mill. Those who had been technical and administrative staff in the mill had skills and experience that made them suitable for similar work elsewhere. Many apparently succeeded in finding new jobs, but much of this information was based on hearsay. Our concern here is what happened to the large majority employed in the spinning or weaving shops or other production departments after they were made redundant. Their search for new employment was driven by the need to provide for their families, and this period of transition was marked by great insecurity. There was no time and little financial breathing space to recover from the loss of their jobs at the cotton mills. Many could not keep their heads above water without borrowing money from relatives or moneylenders or by asking shopkeepers for credit. They did this in the belief that if the mill did not reopen, at least they could look forward to payment of their savings and other money owed to them by their former employers, including their redundancy pay. Those among them who finally did receive their money, considerably less than what they were entitled to, had to use it to pay off the loans and other debts they had run up to survive the period of unemployment.

The search for other work

Having lost their jobs in the formal sector of the economy some of the men decided to go on indefinite strike. As far as they are concerned, searching for work and income has become the business of the other members of their households.

A little less than one third of the ex-mill workers considered themselves unemployable after their dismissal. Half of those interview considered gave their age (over 50) as the main reason for their not being able to go back to work, while a fifth put it down to failing health. The rest said they were willing to work but were unable to find a job. It would be a mistake to take this difference in motivation too literally. Age and ill health may be valid arguments to stop working, but few people who find themselves suddenly unemployed at the bottom of the economy can afford this luxury, which is possible only if other members of the household compensate for the loss in income. In nearly all cases, this proved to have been so, and was the reason why those who claimed to be still seeking work in vain could continue to do so. Unemployment is therefore a flexible concept, determined by what is considered suitable work at any given moment. The final choice, and whether this in turn is eventually revised as a last resort, depends on the balance between the availability of work conditioned by factors such as the nature of the work, levels of workload, respectability and regularity, the pay and the

Ill health is a good enough reason, in the case of older men in particular, for not going in search of other work any longer. But disabled younger males often cannot afford to remain unemployed. Id Mohammed Roz Mohammed, born in Gorakhpur (UP), came to Ahmedabad 22 years ago. He is now 42 and suffers from bysinosis, which he contracted during 20 years of working in the mill. Since his dismissal last year he and his wife are home-based workers, stitching bags for which they are paid according to the quantity produced: two rupees for twelve bags. Even working until late at night his daily income does not rise above Rs. 50.

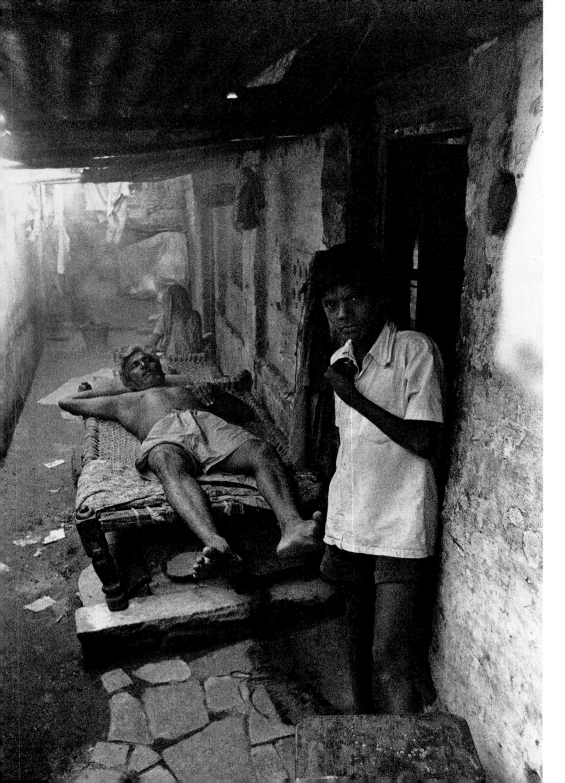

other terms of employment – and the extent to which the obligation to acquire income for the household can be delegated to other members. The starting point in the former mill workers' search for other work was always the same: the desire to find a job that, as far as possible, offered what the mill provided. The absence or inaccessibility of such employment explains why, in most cases, it took so long for them to find new occupation. The period of idleness allowed them to adjust their aspirations to a much lower level. As mentioned above, this adjustment was more difficult for some than for others, while a significant group refused to take a step back at all.

A segregated job market

A minority of former mill workers managed to find jobs close to their earlier line of work. These were mostly Patels, who were taken on elsewhere as weavers. They now work in small powerloom units where, as we shall see, their working conditions are much worse than they were in the mills. Consequently, they tend to change jobs frequently. After redundancy, most of them got their first jobs through other caste members who did the same kind of work. In the same way, dalits who worked together in the mills and now live in the same neighbourhoods, have helped each other find work. This is, however, mostly outside the textile industry because there is almost no demand for the kind of work the workers used to perform in the spinning shops. A handful earn part of their living by hand-spinning at home on the *ambar charkha*. They earn so little that the money is purely a secondary source of income. Surviving discriminatory practices exclude dalits from a wide range of professions. Although they receive preferential treatment in the public sector, private business employers from higher castes seem to avoid employing members of scheduled castes, not least because of their resentment against the government policy of positive discrimination. Another category of workers suffering such handicaps in the search for work are those who were not born and bred in Ahmedabad, or at least in Gujarat. Even after they have lived in the city for many years, their social and work contacts tend to be limited to their own environment. The tendency to keep these 'outsiders' at arm's length is reinforced by their poor command of Gujarati. The restricted social circles in which ex-mill workers from Rajasthan, Uttar Pradesh, Maharashtra, and Andhra Pradesh operate means that they lack the necessary social capital to allow them to move into other sectors. Members of the Muslim minority also find their mobility on the labour market hampered by their social identity. Although other Muslims help them to find work in craft-based occupations, Hindu employers and clients often refuse to make use of their services. Our findings show that the social identities which determined the division of tasks in the mills have also proved the most important channel for finding other work. Caste membership and religious affiliation determine efforts to help others find new employment opportunities. Coincidence and personality have also played its part, of course, but in the choice of what to do or not do, where to look and not look, the workers' caste or communal background has often been of decisive significance.

This open-air glass factory is very labour intensive, but hazardous to health and environment.

Conditions of new employment

The former mill workers would prefer jobs with a permanent contract because of the security and protection provided by such a status; this had ended when they were made redundant. The closest they come to that now is an unwritten and even unspoken contract in which employer and employee agree to continue the relationship until the contract is terminated. This is the basis on which workers are taken on by factories or workshops as wage labourers for an indefinite period, or as guards by companies that specialize in security for industrial premises, offices, or residential quarters. As long as the work they do fulfils the requirements of the employer, they can be sure of a job. But they derive no rights from this employment. Casual labourers, who are taken on daily or until a job is done – an arrangement that is standing practice in the building industry – are in an even more vulnerable position. These people assemble early in the morning at one of the many labour markets (*nakas*) – it may be a road junction, a square, or a bus station – where they wait for the jobbers and subcontractors to come and recruit the labour they need. Sometimes, a relative, neighbour, or friend might have asked them to tag along as an extra hand or may have told them to report directly to the building site. This meeting of supply and demand is not based on legally valid terms of employment and the covert agreement is vague and fluid.

More numerous than these regular and casual wage labourers are those who are self-employed. Three of the most common occupations in this contingent are those of rickshaw drivers, street vendors (of cloth and garments, food and drinks, crockery, vegetables, etc.), and repairmen or recyclers of waste materials. Others work at home, making garments, paper, toys, or plastic articles etc. on a subcontractual basis. Although they are without doubt economically active, they find it difficult to say what their main occupation is. This is also because many of them have to be engaged in several trades to earn enough to keep their heads above water. Then there are those who are active only occasionally. They work on some days and not on others, depending on the demand for their services. They are not overly active in seeking work but do not refuse it if it is offered to them.

At the early morning labour markets, the supply side negotiates with contractors about terms of employment for odd jobs on a daily basis. The former mill hands fall in the category of helpers and are engaged as unskilled workers on construction sites, loading and unloading trucks, repairing roads, digging trenches, etc. Craftsmen carrying their own tools, such as carpenters, painters or plumbers, are paid at least double that of the many more who have only their labour power to sell. Demand is highly seasonal and the assembled crowd is kept waiting for many hours, often in vain. Kalubhai Babubhai Parmar is one of these men. While he was the only income-earning member of the household when he was employed at the mill, he now goes to the nearby morning labour market with his wife every day. They get up at 5 a.m., cook and pack lunch and stand waiting for work in the naka until 11 a.m. If they have not been hired by then, they go back home. Over the years, his wife has sold her ornaments and cut down drastically on expenditure to keep the household going.

Loss of skill and regularity

The ex-mill workers are now employed in jobs that typically require a far lower level of capital investment than did the work they performed in the mills. If mechanized power is involved at all, it is in the form of simple machines: a motor rickshaw, a sewing machine, other simple equipment to repair clocks and watches, radios, bicycles to household articles, or craft tools to produce handmade commodities like leather goods, furniture, *ambar charkhas*, and paintbrushes. Only the weavers in the powerloom sheds work on the same machines that they used in the mills, which have been sold to the owners as scrap. The skill levels outside the industrial sector of the economy is much lower, and it is especially in these branches – small-scale trade, transport, and services – that a large proportion of the former mill workers have ended up. Many of them have lost the skills that they learned in the mills. On the other hand, the work now demands much greater physical effort. Complaints from construction labourers, pedal rickshaw drivers, cart pullers, head porters, and ambulant street vendors about being exhausted at the end of the day must partly be seen in the light of the fact that they now work far less with machines.

The work in the mills had a daily rhythm of eight hours, leaving enough time for workers to spend with the family, do household chores, and engage in activities outside the home. This is now impossible. On paper, powerloom workshops are supposed to operate according to a three-shift roster. As everyone knows, however, the working hours are split up into a day shift and a night shift, each lasting ten to twelve hours. The employers will not take anyone on for less. More is of course always possible. If someone does not turn up for work, a member of the previous shift can simply work another ten or more hours. Home-workers can decide for themselves how many hours they work, but the pressure to earn more by starting early in the morning and working until late in the evening is great. Often all the members of the household play some part in the production, leaving very little leisure time for them to spend together. Others who work in the open air at their own expense can determine the length of their own working day. Street vendors offer their wares long after night has fallen and have to be up and ready to replenish their stocks at the break of day. And then, there is the not inconsiderable number who have to spend part of the day or night doing a second job to supplement their low income. The former mill workers have to cope not only with much longer, but also much more irregular, working hours. Although they used to work in three eight-hour shifts, the shift schedule was drawn up in advance and they were paid extra for overtime. Such bonuses are a thing of the past and the regular cycle of their working lives has been replaced by erratic and unpredictable interruptions and long periods of idleness during which they are not paid. The fact that they show up for work is no guarantee that they will actually be employed on any particular day. It is often uncertain whether the working day will begin at all and how it will develop, and workers are expected to adapt themselves to these large and often unpredictable fluctuations. Free days and leave have become a luxury and are never paid.

Ratanben, widow of ex-mill worker Khushalbhai Parmar. She lives together with her three daughters, her son, her daughter-in-law and two grandchildren. The son works in a factory, where he earns Rs. 35-40 per day. All the women and girls in the house help in the making of incense sticks. They are paid Rs. 100 for 5 bundles of 200 sticks. Working together, four to five females are able to produce on average 400 sticks daily, which means an average income of barely Rs. 10 per head.

Inclusion of women and children in the labour process

More than any other criterion the enormous drop in income illustrates the degree to which the quality of life of the former mill workers has deteriorated. The weavers who now earn their living in small enterprises do the same work, but for much lower pay. Nor can they always be sure that there will be work for them. Most ex-mill workers who earned a daily wage of between Rs. 90 and 100 at the time of closure – at eight hours a day, six days a week, this amounted to between Rs. 2,000 and Rs. 2,500 per month – nowadays earn less than half of that, while a sizeable minority have to make do with less than a third of what they earned before. The fall in income is so dramatic that other members of the household are forced to work. Except for a few workers who had secondary sources of income – as owners of a *pan*-cum-cigarette stall, musicians, barbers, renters of handcarts or rickshaws etc. – the mill was the only source of income on which the household budget was based. The stigmatization of dalits also made it difficult for their wives to find paid work. Muslim women were not permitted to work outside the home, while the higher Hindu castes, such as the Patels, were restricted by similar taboos. The wages brought home by the man of the house was sufficient to allow these customs to be observed or imposed, but after the closure of the mills there was no longer the financial freedom for such sensitivities. Home-working allowed Muslim and some Hindu women to take an active part in earning income for the household without having to break the social code for appropriate public behaviour. Sewing and embroidering clothing, making incense sticks (*agarbati*) and rolling cigarettes (*bidis*) are prime examples of activities in which all household members, particularly women and children, can take part. But in many cases, women and children are also forced to work outside the house. For instance, they may be employed in garment ateliers but may also have to seek work as domestic servants. Collecting paper and other waste (such as scrap metal or empty plastic bottles), which has a low status and earns very little, is the speciality of dalit women and girls.

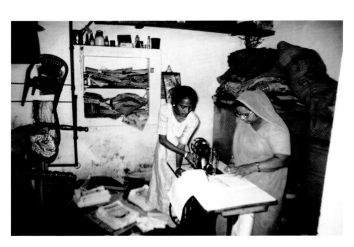

The choice between working at home or outside is often not the prerogative of women themselves but is predetermined by codes of conduct which do not condone female employment or, if this has become inevitable, then at least not beyond the privacy of the house.

While many women from the Other Backward Castes (O.B.C.) can be found selling vegetables in markets and streets, their dalit sisters are domestic servants or move around as scrap collectors, scavengers and rag pickers. This scrap collector is the wife of Khevabhai Maganbhai Chauhan. Since her husband lost his mill job in 1994 she has been doing this work, for which she leaves home daily at 4 a.m.

Contrary to girls, who are made to work alongside their mothers at home or elsewhere, boys learn to become independent street-based operators at a young age.

Fall in living standards

In some of the households of former mill workers, the shortage of income has sometimes become so acute that impoverishment has given way to outright pauperization. Household members can no longer afford to buy the basic necessities to survive. Even in the much larger numbers of households where the fall in earnings has been less severe, it is still hard to make ends meet. As a result of the gap between income and expenditure, the proportion of the household's budget that has to be spent on food is much larger than before and many have been forced to cut back on both the quantity and quality of their daily food consumption. The tradition of celebrating family events with lavish meals and new clothes has been abandoned and little or no money is left for the purchase of consumer durables. However, although the lifestyle of the industrial workers allows few comforts, the large majority of ex-mill workers are connected to electricity and water supplies, and two-thirds have a toilet in or close to the house. A bicycle and a table or ceiling fan are relatively normal and the majority have a radio and a sewing machine. A little under half still enjoy the luxury of a television set or a pressure cooker, purchased in better times. But many have had to sell such valuable possessions, and even more are no longer able to repair them if they break down. About half own the houses they live in. The remaining rent their homes for around 100 to 150 rupees per month. Although many of these tenements are located in what have now become slum districts, this does nothing to impair their value for those who live in them. The quality of the dwellings has, however, suffered across the board, as residents find themselves unable to afford even the most basic of repairs, for example to roofs or walls; and rent, formerly well within their means, has now become an almost unbearable burden.

Coping with impoverishment in the household

Lilaben is the wife of Ranchodbhai Hirabhai Patani. She is not able to work because of bad health. Her husband is now employed as a casual factory hand and earns only Rs. 1,400 per month. The compensation of Rs. 15,000 which he received when his mill shut down had to be spent on daily household needs. Her two daughters and one son are still very young. The problem of buying enough food for the five of them is nagging at her all the time, to the extent that she cannot afford to think of other problems, such as ill health, let alone of how to educate the children and get them settled in marriage.

Many houses have been converted into workshops. In what used to be living space means of production have been installed, which are operated from early morning until late at night by men, women and also children.

A greater threat to the wellbeing of former mill workers and their families than the deterioration in their food intake is the loss of their right to free or cheap medical care. In the past, they were members of the Employees State Insurance Scheme, set up by the government in 1948 for employees of public and private-sector enterprises. ESIS is funded from contributions by employees and employers, while the government also gives a sizeable subsidy. Under the statutes of the scheme, the workers' families are eligible for medical services, which are provided cost-free. ESIS has its own hospitals and neighbourhood clinics, where its own doctors see patients and prescribe medicines. When workers retired or were unable to go on working due to disability, the insurance cover continued for them and their wives, but those who lost their jobs for other reasons were automatically excluded from the scheme. To their great anguish and resentment, this is what happened to the mill workers when they were dismissed. The benefit that the workers derived from their membership of ESIS was much greater than the contribution they paid into the fund and represented not less than 10 to 15 per cent of their salary. Now that they are no longer insured they try to rely on self-help and only call in low-grade doctors and quacks if they have no choice. These medical practitioners, who are often not properly trained, charge much more for a consultation or an injection than the insurance scheme. And for the treatment of stress and other mental problems that arose during and after the redundancy period there is neither the money nor the professional expertize.

When her husband lost his mill job, Ramiben Vitthalbhai started spinning yarn at home and the two of them together now manage to earn Rs. 1000 per month this way. They have two sons who are both employed in a factory, each earning Rs. 500 per month. The wife of the oldest son adds Rs 150 to the household income of Rs 2,150 per month, bringing the average for the five of them to less than Rs 15 a day.

In terms of income, this family is not at all badly off. Sikander Hussein Sheikh owns a rickshaw bought from the compensation money he received when the mill closed in 1996 and with which he earns Rs. 3000 per month. His wife runs a small provision store, set up in what used to be the front room of their house. Their son also drives a rickshaw and contributes the same amount as his father to the household. One daughter and the daughter-in-law help in the shop and with household work. The family has to spend their hours of leisure sitting in front of the shop because there is not enough room inside for them to sit together.

Loss of social capital

The future of the new generation of children is in jeopardy because their schooling is cut short. Parents can no longer afford to invest in improving the life chances of their offspring. Primary school attendance is not affected much but the impact on more advanced education is greater. Apart from the fact that the cost of intermediate and vocational schooling far exceeds the household budget, the labour power of youngsters is a much needed source of income that has to be tapped at an early age. As a consequence, the level of knowledge of the new generation when they enter the labour market at very young age is often lower than that of the mill workers when they started their working lives many years ago.

Former mill workers also worry a great deal about their children's life partners and the cost of marriages. Looking for suitable candidates is time-consuming and assumes that the parents have the opportunity to deliberate carefully on their choice. Financial considerations play a decisive role in the negotiations, which aim to secure the best candidate at the lowest price. In the absence of a reasonable dowry (gifts of money and commodities with which the arrangement is sealed) girls in particular are forced to accept partners who would never have been eligible before. A lower status, not only for the individual but for the whole family, is the price that has to be paid.

Building up reserves needed at times of crises is now completely out of the question; setbacks occur more often and with greater intensity than they did before the mill closures. Initially, the workers could use their redundancy benefits, but these varied greatly in size and many received nothing at all. How was this money used? A small minority managed to deposit at least part in a savings account, and were resolved not to eat into it until the time came for which it was intended – usually for the purchase or future repairs of a house, or for the marriage of sons or daughters. A much larger number indicated that they had to use the money to pay for medical care, urgent home repairs, or the repayment of debts. By far the largest share was spent on day-to-day expenses since, with the difficult adjustment to a lower level of income, this was the only way that the households could meet their recurrent needs. Clearly this situation, in which expense exceeded income, came to an end when the reserves were exhausted. Redundancy payments were far less than most of the workers were entitled to and, moreover, were paid in instalments over an extended period. This explains why workers could not resist the temptation to spend the money as it came in. Most of them therefore clung to their previous way of life and spending pattern for much longer than they were able to afford.

The dramatic fall in the standard of living of the former mill workers undermined their self-confidence. After the shock of being expelled from the mill came the discouraging experience of looking for a new job, accompanied as it was by the loss of skill and a much lower wage. We heard how the men were completely at a loss in the early days following their dismissal. They would not talk for days on end and refused to eat. Their loss of vitality was so great that even the lightest of physical activity was seen as too exhausting. Some stayed at home, others left the house early in the morning and came back late at night, refusing to disclose where they had been or what they had been doing. This state of shock easily led to acute and sometimes severe health problems; such ailments were used as an excuse to

With his redundancy pay Rafiquddin Gyasuddin Sheikh bought this house and took care of the education of his sons. He is now a part-time security guard at Rs. 400 per month. His wife suffers from chronic ill health, has to be looked after constantly by her young daughter and requires medicine which costs Rs. 170 per month. The eldest son (20) is a shop assistant (Rs 1,500 per month) but he cannot work every day because of epileptic fits. His expense on medication is Rs 70 per month. The second son (19) has found employment in an optical company (Rs. 1,800 per month). The third son (16) is still studying at the Industrial Training Institute (ITI) and pays for his own education and maintenance by selling tea. The parents' main worry is about the future of their children. Where will they find the money to pay for them to marry and settle down?

avoid helping with daily household chores. ESIS medical records show an increasing number of patients in the industrial neighbourhoods with heart problems and high blood pressure. The greatest demand was for social care and psychological counselling, but this was not covered by the insurance. Social relationships within the family suffered. Husbands and wives quarrelled, often leading to violence on the part of the man, and sometimes even vice versa. Tensions also increased between parents and children. According to primary and secondary school teachers in the industrial neighbourhoods, children of such families became unruly and 'difficult', had problems concentrating, and complained about troubles at home.

Bharatbhai Kishorbhai Parmar, a rickshaw driver, his wife, who tailors garments at home, and their two children, who help their mother. With a total income of Rs. 4,950 per month they live in relative comfort, but only because all of them contribute to the household budget.

The workload of women in particular has become more burdensome and their main task as household managers has been split up into many roles, some of which are fulfilled simultaneously.

The two sisters sewing garments were forced to leave school when their father became unemployed and told them that they had to start working in order to keep the household going.

Abdul Sattar Safiuddin Shaikh is now casually and part-time employed in several shops, earning a total of Rs. 1,500 on average per month. The compensation he received (Rs. 80,000) enabled him to buy a house but he had to sell this property again in order pay for the treatment of paralysis which he contracted when the mill closed. Due to stress his speech is slurred but he is quite adamant about securing an education for his daughter.

Primary schools, Muslim ones in particular, are forced to run on a much lower budget than before and the number of children enrolled in education has gone down.

Marriage has to be celebrated with pomp and circumstance. But parents cannot afford to spend much on such occasions anymore and music bands face difficulties in finding customers.

Change in gender balance

Little has survived of the men's former claim of being primary providers for their households. After the loss of their permanent jobs and the relatively high wages to which they were accustomed, many feel useless, apathetic, and aggrieved. The other members of the household are expected to show sympathy and understanding for their plight, but as time has passed, sympathy has increasingly given way to irritation at the victims' persistent complaining and inability to accept reality. The need to keep their heads above water demands that they no longer dwell on what has been lost but try and make the best of it. The women, who have always been much more involved in the daily struggle to keep the household going and who learned much earlier that they had to look after others and not just themselves, seem much more able to adjust to the precariousness of the new circumstances than their male partners. It should not be forgotten that they too were affected, not so long ago, by the redundancy that has now so defeated the men. The expulsion of female workers from the mills, however, generated little or no commotion at the time. This was the consequence of new attitudes that came to the fore as the process of industrialization and urbanization progressed. In this 'modern' view, the basic social unit was the nuclear family, with the man as the breadwinner, the woman as wife and mothers and the children as dependent members of the household, exempted from labour.

The ideology of men as the breadwinners explains why they felt ashamed after being made redundant. Their dismissal marks them as failures, not only in their own eyes but also in those of the other household members. The greater resilience of the women in surviving the crisis must be understood in this light. When confronted with their own 'redundancy' in the mills, they were not supposed to have experienced it as a major problem. A large number had to continue their working life, without interruption but less visibly, at home or on the street. In fact it has often been the female members of the household who have shown the men how to find work in the informal sector of the economy, as is the case for those who work at home, such as Muslim women, who sew clothes, or Padmashali women, who make incense sticks. It has become normal for the men to go and collect the raw material from, and return the finished goods to, the contractor, and receive the payment, while the women and children take care of the actual production work. Former mill workers have also become street vendors and are now active in various trades that were formerly the domain of the women. Vaghri women do not not mind men of their own caste selling vegetables, but they do resent their tendency to want to dominate. The men set up shop in the front rows, where the most customers pass, put their wares on a small table so that they are more conspicuous, or park their handcarts so that there is little or no space left for the women.

In this chapter the focus has been on the process of impoverishment and its impact on the household. We now look at how the deterioration in the quality of the lives of the former textile workers has manifested itself beyond the level of the household, and why the dissatisfaction that this has generated has not been expressed in forms of protest and resistance in the textile neighbourhoods.

Ramdev Shriram Kewat complained that his wife, whom he has joined in selling vegetables, has become much more assertive since he lost his mill job.

This man is peeling garlic while his wife is rolling *bidis* (country cigarettes). The balance of power in the household has drastically changed since the men lost their mill jobs and most women had to join in the search for additional income.

While collecting waste, rag pickers and other scavengers have to walk long distances. They sell their harvest of plastic, paper, cloth, iron scrap, etc. to different dealers on the outskirts of the city at the end of the day.

Living in a milieu of misery

No visitor to Ahmedabad can fail to observe the sprawling slums on the east bank of the river, which have spread rapidly over the last few decades. A large segment of the city's population is cramped together in these deprived quarters, exposed to environmental degradation and excluded from the most elementary civic amenities. There is a close link between living in a slum and working in the informal sector of the economy. The tall chimneys marking the industrial landscape have disappeared and the factory compounds, for a century or more congested work-sites with people constantly milling around, are vacated and deprived of their economic significance. The new wastelands, filled with the rubble of demolished buildings, which now dominate this part of the city are no longer surrounded by working class neighbourhoods. The lack of steady employment and a sharp fall in incomes have transformed these habitats of the former mill workforce into slum localities.

The alienation of the ex-mill workers from mainstream society is expressed in their reduced access to public services and institutions, including those that are intended for each and every citizen of Ahmedabad. This state of exclusion is accompanied by a loss of control over the conditions that determine the quality of their lives now and in the future. Market discrimination in how they live and work reinforces the acute sense of deprivation and ensures that they do not enjoy equal opportunities to improve their situation. Members of stigmatized groups naturally seek contact with their own kind – Muslims, dalits and other social minorities exposed to discriminatory practices, both individually and collectively – for mutual support and protection. A life of dependency, however, goes hand in hand

From working class neighbourhoods to slum localities

with restricted choice and downward mobility. Indebtedness forces former mill workers to sell their own labour power and that of other household members and to settle for a lower wage in exchange for an advance payment. Such dependency restricts other options and investment in forms of horizontal solidarity which cuts across primordial loyalties. Ex-mill workers have a compelling need to retreat into their own communal niche and to stay aloof from other social segments.

The retrenched textile workers are not the only inhabitants of the industrial districts to have suffered from the collapse of the large-scale textile mills. The impact on petty trade, services, and transport in the mill areas has been enormous, because demand for the services of a wide variety of shopkeepers, street operators, and craftsmen came predominantly from this leading segment of the working population employed in the formal sector of the economy. Many of their customers have become their competitors. The influx of households expelled from the formal sector has put even greater pressure on the already fragile existence of workers in the informal sector. Competition for work has led to much tension and conflict in both residential areas and the workplace. The process of levelling down to the bottom has become manifest in the spread of squalor and has helped create an atmosphere of undiluted depression.

The alley in which people live is called chali, which means 'walk-through'. But it is only possible to do that during day time, because at night the turned-up cots are stretched out. While the women occupy all space inside the small houses, boys and men have to sleep outside.

► The supply of handcarts and their pullers is much larger then the demand for them.

▶

Women pulling handcarts are a marked feature of the street scene in Ahmedabad.

Cloth is still being sold in the streets of Ahmedabad but not any longer produced in formal sector mills.

▶

A gang of migrant labourers has set up camp here. During the day they are taken away by their jobber on road repair or construction work and nowadays also for demolishing mill buildings. In the evening they come back to cook their meals and sleep.

Grades of vulnerability

From early morning until late in the evening the chalis and side roads are crowded with people. The large majority are males of all ages, lying, sitting or standing in front of their houses or hanging around in small clusters. They take to the streets to kill time because there is not much else for them to do. Women who are not engaged in outside work tend to stay at home, not only because of a code of conduct which does not allow them to move about freely but also because they are more busy than their male partners with all kinds of household chores.

Few labourers in the informal sector of the economy succeed in working more than twenty days a month. Street vendors seem to be the most susceptible to seasonal fluctuations, which prevent them from achieving a fixed rhythm of work. On days when it is raining, cold, or very hot, there is less demand for their services and they have to face a considerable drop in income. Daily wage earners are similarly affected. On such days, they will go to the various labour markets in the city where workers are hired early in the morning, only to be turned away. It is the same story at the building sites, where they seek work as unskilled hands. It would, however, be incorrect to attribute the unpredictable nature of work in the open air purely to inclement weather; such work may also by interrupted by public holidays, or by disturbances of the public order, such as riots or political tensions. Seasonal swings in the city's economy, caused by not-so-transparent flows of industrial and mercantile capital in the informal sector, have a greater impact on the mass of workers in this sector than on their counterparts in the better-regulated formal sector; however, not much is known about the nature and effects of these cyclical and erratic trends. They also affect home-workers, whose way of earning a living is completely concealed from public view. The fact that they are apparently available for work at all times does not mean that they have work all the time. The delivery of raw materials is irregular, the power supply is unreliable, and contractors pass on fluctuations in demand for the end product without the slightest scruples.

The large amount of time not spent in gainful work does not mean that this vast reserve army enjoys the many and erratic hours of non-activity at their disposal. Leisure used to be a familiar notion that grew out of the pattern of regular employment in the mill. When they were not on night shift the men would congregate in small groups after the evening meal and sing devotional songs or just engage in small talk together on street corners. Going alone or with the whole family to the Sunday market on the riverbank or to visit relatives living in other neighbourhoods were favourite outings during the weekend. Those days are gone. Although there is more 'idle time' available now, there is neither money nor energy to enjoy it as leisure.

Not all workers who have lost their mill jobs have fallen below the poverty line. There are those who do not have to rely solely or predominantly on the sale of their unskilled labour power. These include the owners of petty means of production – such as motorized rickshaws, handcarts, or street cabins – or of parcels of land, or small buildings in slum areas, who not only use this property themselves but rent or lease it out. Although the percentage of workers having access to various forms of petty capital should not be exaggerated, their households are certainly better off than those who have no means of production themselves. At the opposite end of the spectrum,

Rajubhai Mangabhai Patni has, in the local parlance, 'gone mad' since losing his mill job. His aged mother is taking care of him. Both depend for their livelihood on what his brother, who has his own family to support, can afford.

there is an extremely vulnerable segment of ex-mill workers who, because of ill fortune or disability, are alienated from both the means of production and consumption. The households to which they used to belong have broken up. There are instances of men deserting their wives and children, unwilling to provide for them any longer, but there are also cases of men being thrown out of their houses soon after losing their jobs at the mill. Such people, the ultra-excluded, roam the streets as lost souls, begging and afflicted by acute pauperization. They depend for their irregular and inadequate meals on *ramroti,* centres of free food distribution run by religious charities.

Farid Miya was told by his wife and children to leave the house because he could not provide for them once he lost his job. Due to the disease which he contracted after mill closure – his hands never stop shaking – he cannot work anymore and now lives with his sister.

This man's son committed suicide because of lack of suitable employment prospects.

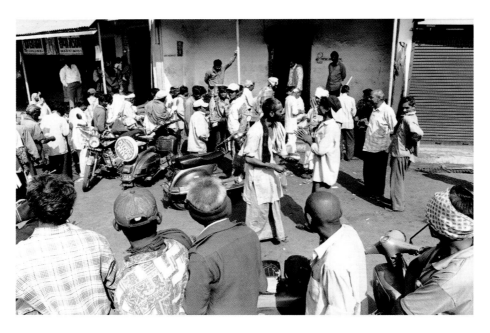

Ramroti run by Jalaram Sewa Mandal, a religious charity.

Erosion of public space

There is another source of income for people forced to live in the informal sector, which gives a small percentage a larger income than would figure in official records: a wide range of criminal activities, such as theft and fencing, robbery and extortion, distilling and smuggling liquor, trading in weapons or drugs, gambling, the prostitution of women and children or touting for them, and the use of violence against persons for payment. The distinction between self-employment and casual or regular wage labour also applies to these practices. Those working on their own account and at their own risk may combine such work with membership of gangs hired on a regular or incidental basis, by landlords and slum bosses to drive out squatters, by politicians to intimidate opponents or to persecute minorities, and by criminals to even scores with other criminals. The scale of the work provided and the income generated in this way should not be underestimated, in an economy where more than half the total money circulation takes place outside the control of the legal-administrative machinery. It may not be an easy life, given the risks involved, but it is either that or sinking far below the poverty line. Fired mill workers expressed fears that their sons – who, like them, are forced to live at a much lower level of subsistence – would succumb to the temptation of the easy pickings offered by a career of crime. While taking stock of the large range of illegitimate activities, it should not be forgotten that informal sector workers are not only the hunters but also the hunted. The fact that, for most households, total earned income falls short of their basic needs does not mean that they are exempt from all kinds of illegal extortion, including raids from the formal sector to relieve such easy prey of

a part of their income. Here, too, numbers and figures are mere speculation and cannot really express the nature and scale of these levies.

Slum life is characterized not only by signs of want, deprivation, and neglect, the closure of the mills has also led to a shrinking of public space in the settlements surrounding them. Places where people used to meet their workmates and others with different social identities are nowadays difficult to find. Certainly, in the past, too, the mill hands used to spend most of their time off in or around the home, mainly within the confines of the particular communal circle to which they happened to belong. Life-cycle events or religious festivals were public functions which were largely celebrated in the open. The neighbourhood schools run by the municipality were a point of contact where children not only demonstrated the skills picked up within the intimacy of family life on how to deal with 'others', but where they also made friends from the other side of the fence. People living nearby were invited to share in the food and fun, even if they observed other customs themselves. There were clubs which gave training in wrestling, boxing, and other sports to all comers, irrespective of their caste or communal background. And the spectators at the matches were equally mixed.

The reading rooms set up by the TLA throughout the industrial districts were also important meeting places. Classes were held in the mornings and evenings to teach reading and writing to adults and to those who had dropped out of school at an early age. Later, many of these centres were taken over by the Labour Welfare Board, an official agency set up under the auspices of the municipal government. In recent years several of these places have closed down for lack of funds. The municipal corporation decided to cut down on social expenditure and the clientele has dwindled. Apart from the inability of the clients, men as well as women, to pay the very modest fee charged for the various courses or for the crèches where toddlers can be left a few hours each day, they have also lost their appetite for spending 'free' hours in constructive activities. Their time is eaten up in the search for work or in just remaining 'idle'. Venturing out in mainstream society has become an option which many households in the milieu of ex-mill workers can no longer afford.

The Sarangpur Cotton Mill has gone but the bus stop carrying that name is still there.

Cattle and waste collectors roam around in the former industrial grounds. Both do so illegally because the mill owner has engaged a security guard with instructions to chase away trespassers and squatters.

 After mill closures, life naturally goes on and the kite-flying festival on January 14th, Makar Sankranti, is celebrated as keenly as ever.

Downward mobility

Without exception, the ex-mill workers describe their current situation as 'miserable' in comparison with their former life. Were they, despite their subordinate position at the base of the hierarchy in the textile mills, an aristocracy among the working population of Ahmedabad? The use of this term can easily lead to an exaggerated image of the comforts the industrial vanguard previously enjoyed in terms of welfare, security, and protection. This view requires immediate modification given, for instance, the industrial diseases that affected the health of the workforce sooner or later. Many suffered from bysinossis, a disease of the lungs caused by the inhalation of cotton dust, which particularly affected those involved in the initial stages of the production process. Doctors treated the complaint as tuberculosis and the trade union refused to hold the mill owners responsible for the consequences – partial and eventually full incapacity to work.

Whilst accepting that the prevailing conditions in the mills left much to be desired, the workers themselves are apt to consider their dismissal from the mill as a fall from paradise. This opinion says more about the shortcomings of the miserable situation they now find themselves in than how glorious things used to be. More typically different than the length of the working day – much longer than in the mill – is the irregular rhythm of the work and, consequently, the fluctuating income it brings. While the demands on their labour power can sometimes be extremely strenuous and lengthy, there are long spells – hours, days, and even weeks – of enforced idleness. In the words of some of them: 'There is no longer a steady pattern to our lives.' Those who have been lucky to find a regular job have to make do with half or even less of the salary they were paid in the mill. The majority earn less

Loss of security, dignity, and representation

Privacy is beyond the reach of people living in poverty. They are denied the comfort of retreating into the intimacy of the house and the family for such day-to-day activities as washing up or taking a bath.

than the statutory minimum for unskilled labour established by the government of Gujarat for a large number of trades and industries in the informal sector of the economy. The fall in income is closely related to the shift from a time-wage to piece-rate or job work. This has affected not only those who are self-employed but workers across the board, and led to forms of self-exploitation, such as extending the working day and forcing dependent members of the household to work, at home or outside, whenever and wherever required to do so.

◀ ▼

For lack of employment prospects, the male inhabitants of the erstwhile mill localities spend a lot of time doing nothing. While the women are kept busy in and around the house, the men hang out in the streets during daytime as well as at night.

The price of informalization

The earlier pattern of employment provided the regularity, stability, security and dignity that accompany work in the formal sector of the economy. What was long seen as a logical and attractive model to follow has increasingly been interpreted in negative terms by policy makers, as an unjust form of preferential treatment resulting in a better way of life for a small part of the working class. What used to be considered a vanguard, against the background of a trend towards the economic and more general social emancipation of people who mostly own little more than their labour power, is now seen as a parasitical force. Abolition of the privileges enjoyed by labour in the formal sector is called for, not only on grounds of social justice but also to remove an obstacle to the acceleration of economic growth.

It would definitely be incorrect to attribute this change in the political climate and the economic policy that underlies it to the impact of the process of globalization. By far the majority of the working population in south Asia has always been excluded from the protection provided by the labour legislation introduced in anticipation of the gradual transition from an agrarian-rural to an industrial-urban society. But what is difficult to deny is that, partly under pressure from transnational agencies that operate on the basis of the hegemony of capital over all other factors of production, the earlier pledge to improve the quality of working life step-by-step through public regulation has been abandoned. The post-colonial social history of the state of Gujarat shows that what was intended to be a gradual process of formalization of employment foundered long before the ideology of globalization started to determine the direction of economic policy. The expulsion of the industrial vanguard in Ahmedabad from its position of economic security can be seen as the logical consequence of, first, the abandonment and then the reversal of this process.

Those who praise informalization as the solution for unemployment tend to overlook the fact that it is not only founded on a desire to minimize labour costs; of no less importance is the fact that it also offers the possibility of evading taxes and other levies imposed by the government. In that sense, the process of informalization that extends to the economy as a whole and entails freeing capital from the constraints of official regulation. Thanks to the policy of liberalization that has been pursued since as far back as the 1970s, Gujarat is one of the fastest growing states in India. It has achieved this distinction on the basis of a path of 'development', described by its proponents as a combination of dynamic entrepreneurship, a government with the political will to give private business a free rein, and what is seen by vested interests as 'a favourable labour climate'. These praises tend to ignore the disastrous effects of this strategy on the social balance as well as on the environment. Pollution has reached alarming levels in the industrial zones of the city, the effects of which are expressed in the rising morbidity of the people who live and work in them.

The flexibilized working population which dominates the economy of Ahmedabad has all the characteristics of a floating reserve army. Whole contingents are hired and fired by industrial and mercantile capital according to the dictates of the moment. As a result, in the daily struggle to survive, this marginalized mass is condemned to perpetual mobility in the search for work, both within and between sectors of employment. Confined in their status of reserve labour, this extremely vulnerable segment maintains its own reserve – the dependent members of their households. Out of public view, it is usually the weakest and smallest shoulders that have to bear the heaviest burdens of informalization. The image of shared poverty does not do justice to the inequality with which this form of existence at the urban bottom is permeated, within the sphere of the household.

Not many ex-mill workers can be found reading books or newspapers. Their interest in politics or in what is going on in society at large has reduced and most reading rooms which were run by the Textile Labour Association have closed down.

Leisure has become a luxury although not for lack of time. Going to the Sunday market on the river bank used to be a popular outing for the mill workers. They came with their family to buy household utensils or toys for the children but nowadays cannot afford any longer to do so.

The municipal council has cut down on public activities in the working class localities. The Labour Welfare Board has stopped the funding for many programmes and many parents cannot afford even the small fees charged for sending infants to nursery school or to allow teenagers to participate in low-cost sports and games. Children are back to playing in the streets of their own neighbourhood.

Dis-organization

Was there no resistance to this far-reaching restructuring of the labour regime? The dismantling of the large-scale textile industry in Ahmedabad was a process that unfolded over a period of many years, during which time at no point were the victims able to mount a sustained or concerted protest. The dominant mood was one of bitterness and resentment. The trade union, which could have channelled these frustrations into organized action, was prevented from doing so by a doctrine that preached industrial harmony, and a willingness to make concessions and seek compromises at all times. This ideology explains why the TLA failed to take decisive action when the mills closed down. The Gandhian strategy to which the union leaders adhered from the very beginning had undeniably produced many benefits for its members, not least because of the political influence the union wielded both in Gujarat and nationally. In addition to higher wages, this high-powered lobby resulted in significant industrial legislation and a tripartite framework for its implementation. But at the critical hour, when they should have insisted that the agreements be honoured, the leaders made a conscious decision not to mount an orchestrated campaign against the mass redundancies, thereby abandoning the rights for which earlier generations of the industrial workforce had fought. The Gandhian union accepted as inevitable the expulsion of the huge workforce from the formal sector of the economy.

The management of the new high-tech industrial enterprises on the outskirts of the city often reject applications from former mill workers, saying that they are overage and worn out and therefore lack the flexibility to adapt to the high pace of work. The old hands have become as obsolete as when the women of an earlier generation were driven out of the mills. Today's industrialists prefer younger and fitter workers. Also, the owners of powerloom workshops often refuse to hire victims of mill closure, even though they are better equipped to operate the machines than newcomers with no experience, because of the way these old hands assert themselves.

This woman has for long been an active member of Lal Vavta, a militant trade union strongly critical of the Gandhian approach followed by the TLA.

What is clearly lacking nowadays is the capacity of workers to improve their lot through collective bargaining. The small-scale and fenced off niches that dominate the informal sector landscape present an obstacle to the emergence of organized initiatives to articulate and represent interests within, let alone between, branches of industry. Bargaining for individual favours is considered preferable to acting as a spokesman for others in claiming alleged rights. Demonstrations of assertiveness can be enough to qualify for instant dismissal. Other than the quality of the work performed, the extent to which an employer sees an employee as obedient and essentially docile is an important criterion in hiring, promoting, demoting and firing. Former mill workers are now engaged in types of employment that have led them to be dispersed over a highly diverse and variable pattern of activities and workplaces. Such large-scale fragmentation is a significant obstacle to efforts aimed at collective action.

Our conclusion that the TLA leaders betrayed the trust of the union's members is based not only on the fact that they proved neither willing nor able to direct the protest of the mill workers during the mass redundancies. What happened after they had failed at the critical moment to oppose the closure of the mills and the retrenchment of the workforce without due compensation was indicative of an even greater blunder: they decided that dismissal from the mill also meant that workers lost their union membership. The former members did not even have a chance to cancel their own participation. Collection of their contributions was stopped once mill wages were no longer paid and their names were scrapped from the members' list. The issue was never discussed at a union meeting. Instead of taking a stand for the workers as they were ejected from the formal sector of the economy, the union bosses left them to their fate. This is how the workers themselves see what happened: they were not disloyal to the union; it was the other way around.

Former mill workers still come to the TLA office to enquire about the compensation money which most of them failed to get. The fortunate ones who did receive their gratuity benefits and other dues had to pay a commission of two per cent to the union. Moreover, members of the administrative staff pocketed a part of the money to which the workers were entitled.

The regular union business has come to a halt. The huge building stands empty with hardly any staff around, many rooms are locked and no meetings are held anymore. A few over-aged leaders are still presiding over an organisation which has become defunct.

The righteous struggle in retrospect

Although strikes and other forms of militancy are not rare, they are usually sudden, fragmented, and more or less spontaneous eruptions of protest. Such acts of resistance are restricted to localized disputes, flaring up and dissipating again as abruptly as they started. The incapacity to express solidarity systematically rather than sporadically is a consequence of the segmented and highly volatile nature of the new labour regime.

Together with the changed mode of employment, the state of dire poverty of the majority of people who operate in the informal sector presents an obstacle to collective action. They lack the time, space, or reserves necessary to make demands together with those who share their fate. The dismissed mill workers have not only been forced into deprivation in material terms. Having to agree to a regime of exploitation and subordination as a result of their loss of job security is an extremely heavy burden to bear. And it means having to leave behind the self-respect that was such a significant part of their social consciousness as mill workers and trade union members.

Unable to comprehend why they were expelled from the formal sector of the economy, the former mill workers in Ahmedabad feel disillusioned and alienated. Some of the victims of the policy of informalization have been unable to accept their fate and have sought 'early retirement'. In effect, they have decided to go on indefinite strike. But the awareness still exists that their former assertiveness was a product of the social struggle they had fought. The memory of this time explains why their anger at the inactivity of the TLA at the time of the closures is mixed with nostalgia for the way in which, in better times, the union had assured them of dignified work and life.

Baburao Ganu Telange, lost his job on 31 March 1994, a fateful date imprinted on his mind as if it happened only yesterday. He is now employed as a security guard. After closure the owner sold the remaining stock of cloth as well the machinery and the land on which the mill is standing. All these transactions were illegal and although the workers have jointly filed a case against their erstwhile employer, they have received no compensation at all. This bone of contention still brings them together every third Saturday morning. Inside the compound of the Tata Advance Mill they assemble at the temple which was built many years ago with the donations of the workers to commemorate the 100th anniversary of the mill founded by Jamshedji Tata. They come to discuss the progress of the court case and sing devotional songs (bhajan mandali). Among them is one Muslim for whom they collected enough money to enable him to go to the haj.These workers participate in the meetings not so much to kindle their hopes for compensation but, more meaningfully, to talk about the good old days, and to relive the solidarity which bonded them.

The downfall of this once so mighty representative of organized labour seems imminent. In the old city centre, the imposing union building looks deserted. Gone are the glorious days of mass meetings and union power with which the city's captains of industry were confronted. A bronze sculpture above the entrance to the Gandhi Majoor Sevalaya depicts the way in which the 'righteous struggle' was fought: two mill workers, a man and a woman, look up with adoration at the Mahatma as he points the way to a shining industrial future. The few aged union leaders who have remained semi-active argue among themselves about who bears the greatest responsibility for the decline and fall of their life's work. Every day, they still come for a few hours to the office to meet workers who have not yet given up hope of receiving the compensation to which they are entitled but which has not been paid. When we asked what was going to happen now, we received no answer. Might it not have been possible for the sacked workers to remain members of the TLA ? No, said the General Secretary, a man in his late eighties, because without factories there is no need for trade unions.

His Hindu mates with whom he used to work together donated small amounts to pay for his pilgrimage to Mecca.

Renewed trade unionism

The Self Employed Women's Association (SEWA) tells a different story. Ela Bhatt, the founder of this organization for working women at the base of the urban economy, started her long career when she joined the TLA staff in 1955. As head of the department responsible for providing the wives of the mill workers with information on child care and housekeeping, she became aware of how women were accustomed to work at home to help generate income for the family. This experience made her critical of her role within the union – which involved educating her clients to be good mothers and housewives. In 1972 she was given permission to set up a union for women within the TLA. On her initiative a bank was established to meet the desperate need for credit among the members, whether self-employed or working for wages. In her daily routine Elaben encountered discrimination against mill workers from the lowest caste. This reinforced her belief in the value and necessity of the hotly debated reservation policy, which included various measures to promote upward mobility of members belonging to the scheduled and backward castes. Her strong opinions were not shared by the TLA top leaders and in 1981, after she had expressed her support for continuation of this public policy in a mass meeting, she fell into disfavour. The union leaders broke all ties with her and SEWA. Now, with the TLA on the verge of folding up, SEWA is thriving. In Ahmedabad alone, it has a membership of 55,000 working women, who make use of the services it provides, such as credit, health facilities, life insurance, and legal aid. By the end of 2000 membership in Gujarat had risen above 200,000, more than the TLA ever enlisted in the state. The women who were expelled from the mills in the previous generations can rightly be seen as the present-day torchbearers of the 'righteous struggle' that Gandhi launched in the early years of the last century to improve the lot of the industrial workers. SEWA has also organized the protests of street vendors against their eviction from public space. A few years ago Ela Bhatt and her staff achieved one of their greatest successes when the ILO adopted a convention for the protection of homeworkers.

The bronze relief above the entrance to the TLA office depicts Gandhi showing the masses which have become redundant in the agrarian economy, the road to a better industrial future. Below him a female and a male worker look up to their patron in grateful adoration.

Elaben Bhatt in the mid-fifties when she joined the TLA. She was given charge of women's activities but soon found out that catering to their economic needs was much more relevant and urgent then improving their performance as housewives.

SEWA members celebrating the outcome of their struggle over public space. They have just won to the right to sell vegetables on the pavement of Ahmedabad.

These women belong to the neighbourhood-based cadre of SEWA.

Communal versus class identities

The sustained policy of the Indian trade union movement not to mobilize informal sector workers should be judged as a historic blunder. Timely acknowledgement of the organic linkage between formal and informal sectors of the economy would have made it possible to co-opt the labouring poor in the struggle to promote the rights of all segments of the working class in a balanced manner. A programme that focused on more than just a small segment of the total workforce could have prevented the agents of organized labour from becoming seemingly helpless bystanders in the on going onslaught of informalization which has eroded whatever political strength they might have had in the past.

There have been some remarkable exceptions, however, to the general decline of the formal labour movement. In various parts of India social activists aligned to different political parties have successfully campaigned for a minimum of socioeconomic security for men and women in the informal sector of the economy. What at one stage seemed to be swimming against the tide may very well become a new model for facilitating the emancipation of fragmented and subaltern segments of the working population. In representing the interests of the labouring poor, the new movements have to draw up an agenda which distinguishes them from conventional trade unions which cater only to members higher up in the employment hierarchy.

Social ties based on principles other than class solidarity play a leading role in the articulation of identities in the economy of the informal sector. Caste and faith operate as signposts in seeking and finding work. Entitlement to favours and protection or support in the event of misfortune are also

A city torn apart

channelled along these lines. Such forms of social inclusion take on the character of networks based on primordial bonds without emerging neatly structured associations. This explains why they often remain invisible to outsiders. The suggestion that these are forms of false consciousness overemphasizes their ideological aspect, whilst denying the practical significance of caste and religion to the way in which people try to reduce their vulnerability in daily life. Such identities also permit collective action, in situations in which class-based assertiveness might be subject to all kinds of social restrictions. This is how we should also understand the strength of segmentary movements which call on their followers to free themselves from a situation of repression and deprivation. But, in contrast to the emancipatory élan that these social movements display, there is also the fact that mobilization of such formations for political and economic objectives occurs at the expense of breaking through horizontal dividing lines, or may even reinforce them. Strengthening identities within a closed community can shift the focus of attention away from solidarity with 'others'. Short-range engagement prevents the search for bonding with others who share the same fate on the basis of a social perspectives inspired by the struggle for a better existence for all those who live in poverty.

This is a signification reason why the strategic choices made by SEWA in Ahmedabad merit attention. The union is aware of the diverse identities of its membership, the large majority of whom come from subaltern Hindu castes and the Muslim minority. But the starting point for the programme of activities is not their differences but the interests they share: their position as working women and as residents of deprived neighbourhoods or slums. In the informal sector, loyalties based on restricted associational networks retain their power because of the clear benefits to those who belong to them.

Next to work, gender and locality can be seen as examples of identities which are catalysts for collective action. Adopting these as guiding principles for mobilization at the grassroots level encourages a feeling of solidarity that helps to break through more restrictive communal barriers. The success of this formula depends on the ability of the SEWA leadership to bring up its grassroots cadre to senior staff positions and on the understanding, both at the top and among the rank and file, that their struggle is not only for economic gains but also to build up political power in the fight for justice.

While in the past wrestling and boxing were popular sports in working class neighbourhoods, these clubs nowadays have become recruitment ground for the storm troops of communal forces. At the outbreak of a new pogrom, lumpenized youngsters from the slums are aroused to do the looting, burning, and killing.

The only shop not burnt in this row has a non-Muslim owner.

Most Hindus, like this man, who have lost their property belong to the lower castes.

The return of social darwinism

At the end February and in early March 2002, violence once again erupted in Ahmedabad, on this occasion on a scale and intensity that far surpassed that of previous rounds. The escalation occurred largely because the BJP state government provided no protection for the victims of persecution, but gave its supporters a free hand – and even encouraged them – in their witch-hunt against the members of the religious minority. Eyewitnesses like Kapilaben, a SEWA grassroots worker, have narrated their nightmarish experience of the violence and counter-violence;

What can I tell you? I have seen terrible scenes – everything happened in front of my eyes. I have seen mobs of 4,000 to 5,000 men stalking the city with guns and swords, burning and looting. I have seen one man's hands cut off, another's stomach ripped open and intestines hanging out. I have also seen the police actively participating in all of this. I have seen the dead and injured lying on the road with no first aid. I have seen death, blood, suffering, fear – I have seen things like never before. I can never forget what I witnessed. When I visited Ambikanagar, a Hindu community, there was nothing there; everything had been razed to the ground. It was the same for Mariam bibi ki Masjid, a Muslim area. Not a single hut was left. All we could see were the charred remains of the house and the belongings strewn about. I sat down and cried, how can we rebuild after such destruction?

Like many women who are members of this informal-sector trade union, Kapilaben lives in a part of the city where the textile mills used to be located.

Seeking shelter in one of the refugee camps with all that the victims were able to save from their earthly belongings.

It is indicative of the scale of the violence that raged in the former textile neighbourhoods that, of the more than 55,000 women who are members of SEWA in Ahmedabad, 38,000 were victims, to a greater or lesser extent, of the wave of anger and hatred that lasted for several weeks; 21,900 of them were forced to flee to one of the 46 camps set up to provide emergency shelter.

Registration of widowed victims.

The residents of the slum localities were not only the victims of the communal rage and hatred, they also responded *en masse* to the call to eliminate the members of the opposing group. The main targets of the violence were the Muslims, many hundreds of whom – men, women and children – were killed, often in the most horrific ways. The pogrom made it clear that the Sangh Parivar organizations constituting the Hindutva movement had succeeded in inciting the lumpen army of unemployed and semi-unemployed youth in the industrial districts to participate in the spree of murder, looting and arson. In an early report on these events, based on a short visit to the sites of my fieldwork, I made a link between the stark impoverishment and degradation of the industrial neighbourhoods as an outcome of the mill closures and the pogroms which took place largely in these localities. The communal tolerance that once existed has gone. When the mills were still open, the workers also lived in nearby colonies divided according to caste and faith. These were small-scale clusters no larger than a few chalis or blocks of houses. The Other was not at

Abdul Sattar and his wife have two sons and five daughters. The mill where he worked closed ten years ago. His present boss sent him home when the violence began and he does not know if he can go back there. The whole family went to the relief camp when the riots continued. The inhabitants of the Hindu locality in which his house is located do not want them to come back and he does not know what to do now.

a distance but highly visible and touchable as a workmate, a customer, a neighbour, or a friend, with whom close contact was maintained both within and outside the mill. The close-knit community feeling which used to exist lives on in the tales about what has been lost: memories of visits to one's neighbours, to share in the joys and sorrows of family life, to pay their respects or to show each other hospitality on festive occasions, to share the burden of everyday problems. This mesh of social cohesion that transcended the niches of separate identity broke down once the mills had closed, the TLA started to fade away and municipal agencies, due to lack of funding, had to cease or drastically curtail their welfare activities. The climate of social darwinism that replaced it not only established the right of the survival of the fittest, but meant that the most vulnerable at the base of society were forced to compete with each other as hunter and hunted. My report describes the difference between past and present civic upheaval:

'No doubt, there were communal disturbances also then. When riots broke out in 1969 the police agreed to set up a control room at the headquarters of the trade union and, on the basis of messages received by phone from its cadre in the mill localities, the leadership kept the authorities informed about the latest incidents. The factories had stopped production but on the third day of the riots the call came for members of the TLA to report back to duty. Workers of the same shift but with different caste and religious identities were told to go to the mills and back home in mixed batches in order to safeguard each other's well-being. Nowadays there is hardly any space left for that sort of intercommunal sharing and mutual protection. The union, which at that time was one of the largest and best organized in the country, is a spent force, reduced to less than one tenth of its former strength and depleted from all economic and political power. In mid-March 2002, with parts of the city still under curfew, I met the Secretary-General in his office, a big building once vibrant with activity but which now stands desolate in the heart of the old city. This veteran, at the age of 88 years and in failing health, told me with anguish how a fortnight ago he had endeavoured for many hours to reach the police commissioner as well as prominent politicians. When he received no response to his incessant calls on 28 February, he realized that the state machinery deliberately refused to give shelter to the victims and to protect life and property when the rampage of killing and looting was at its worst. In the relentless drive towards a regime of informality as the dominant mode of employment, labour appears to have forfeited not just its economic value, bargaining power, and dignity. In vain this Gandhian stalwart had tried to persuade his office staff, cut down from its former impressive size to a few helpers, to come along with him on a tour of the industrial localities in order to pacify the incited mob. In addition to their blunt refusal to go out into the streets they also warned him against risking his life on such a hopeless mission.'

Mohammed Yunus was a weaver and started repairing bicycles in a cabin when he lost his mill job. During the latest riots his house in Bapunagar was destroyed in front of his eyes and he and his family had to seek shelter in this camp.

Mustaq Ahmed was a badli worker when the mill closed in 1988. Since then he has been a rickshaw driver but could not afford to buy his own vehicle. All his savings were spent on the purchase of a house in Bapunagar. The house was cheap because it stands on the border between a Muslim and a Hindu zone. Four of the six houses in this row have been burnt. Fortunately, his property was not among them, but looters broke in and took away all the valuables which they could carry. Relatives gave him some money to buy new utensils and soon he and his family hope to leave the relief camp and to go back home.

In the wake of the riots, SEWA was one of the few civic organisations which immediately started relief work. In addition to providing shelter, food and other basic requirements the camp staff made arrangements for the refugees to earn an income. The women were employed in making garments and the children in recycling waste paper into bags.

Abdul Karim Fatehmud standing in front of his gutted and burnt-out shop in Gomtipur, near Mariam Bibi Masjid, one of the worst affected localities in the riots. He does not know where to find the money to restart his work as a tailor but, with a loan from the company, at least his STD (public phone) booth is back in business again.

When Lallu Bhil lost his mill job he started a tea stall, which gave him an income of 40 to 50 rupees a day. His lari was destroyed in the violence but he intends to buy a new one from the compensation which the government has promised to pay to the victims. There were many Muslims among his customers and Lallu is sure that they will come back to him again.

Many Muslim victims of the riots are often not allowed to go back to their own locality. Driven out by neighbours they are forced to flee to another part of the city where they can settle down among members of their own community. Sanklit Nagar, in Juhapura, is one of the slums in which Muslims have come to live during the last decade. In the middle-class Hindu quarters of Ahmedabad this ghetto is known, and hated, as mini Pakistan.

Politics of exclusion

In the wake of the communal riots which swept through the mill localities in 1969, the TLA leadership invited Khan Abdul Badshah Khan, better known as the 'Frontier Gandhi', to visit Ahmedabad. In the Jumma Masjid he called for reconciliation and criticized those who used their own faith to persecute others who thought differently. His speech was reprinted in *Majoor Sandesh* in March 2002. When I left Ahmedabad at the end of that month, order and peace had not yet been restored in the city. The curfew was lifted in some parts of the city, only to be reimposed the next day in the same or other localities because of new incidents. There has been hardly any discussion of what all this meant for the large number of working class households who fully depend on the erratic and meagre yield of their labour power. Even under so-called normal circumstances steady employment is difficult to come by, but for more than three weeks at a stretch they had not able to move around in their cumbersome search for gainful work. For many of them the regular state of deprivation in which they live has further deteriorated into destitution. Without any food left and bereft of all creditworthiness, they have to survive on whatever private charities are willing to dole out to them.

With a few exceptions, the institutions that represent civic society took no action at all when the communal riots and the horrific violence that accompanied them broke out. Ahmedabad citizens are proud of the large number of non-governmental agencies located in the city. In the past, commentators have widely praised their role in development. These efforts have, however, reaped few concrete benefits for the poorer parts of the population, and for the large number of Muslims among them in particular. For collective action, the city's excluded minority have always been, and

remain, dependent on charity in their own circle. In the pauperized industrial localities of Ahmedabad 'the righteous struggle', which did succeed in generating a certain amount of crossborder solidarity , lives on only in the memory of a better past.

As in earlier pogroms, pamphlets were circulated urging people (meaning Hindus) not to buy from Muslims or employ members of that community, but to avoid all business transactions with them. In the Sangh Parivar mindset, the members of the minority community have become the new untouchables of Gujarat.

A welfare state which provides ample social security from the cradle to the grave may also have become a closed chapter in the recent history of West European societies. This does not mean to say, however, that the social awareness that has been aroused through a long process of emancipation should unavoidably be subordinated to the unbridled interplay of economic supply and demand in the accelerating process of globalization. The price for that, expressed in the emergence of new inequalities in and outside the labour market, is too high. Social care arrangements should be insisted upon, if only to build up the countervailing power needed to mitigate the harmful impact of employment insecurity. Regulation by the government and restriction of the free market mechanism are necessary to put an end to the exclusion from a decent standard of work and life of the huge and still growing army of labour in the informal sector, which is in many respects used as a reserve. To ensure that a coolie class of untouchables does not congest at the broad base of the world economy, including or rather excluding a considerable proportion of humanity, an extensive programme of social security is urgently required.

While the districts on the left bank of the Sabarmati, where the mills and their workforce were located, have deteriorated into slums, the new Ahmedabad on the right bank of the river is booming. The erstwhile captains of industry have reinvested their money in real estate, which they found more profitable than running the textile mills. The riots mainly took place on the other – the 'bad' side of the river.

Skyscrapers and luxurious bungalows are the habitat of the rapidly expanding middle class. People living here have not been bothered much by the riots but Muslim houses and business establishments, which had been identified in advance, were singled out for looting and burning by lumpen gangs sent to these targets.

The shopping malls, beauty saloons, fast food cafeterias, internet cafes, billboards, high-fly offices and bank branches all cater to the lifestyle of the newly rich. It is a world apart from the space inhabited by the ex-mill workers. In these zones of prosperity they are merely tolerated as security guards, domestic helpers, street vendors, scavengers and waste collectors.

A cup of coffee or a soft drink in one of these fashionable places is equal to half or more the daily wage of an ex-mill worker.